Economics of the Iroquois

BY

SARA HENRY STITES

University Press of the Pacific
Honolulu, Hawaii

Economics of the Iroquois

by
Sara Henry Stites

ISBN: 1-4102-2015-X

Reprinted from the 1905 edition

University Press of the Pacific
Honolulu, Hawaii
http://www.universitypressofthepacific.com

In order to make original editions of historical works available to scholars at an economical price, this facsimile of the original edition of 1905 is reproduced from the best available copy and has been digitally enhanced to improve legibility, but the text remains unaltered to retain historical authenticity.

CONTENTS.

INTRODUCTION.

Sketch of the Economic Systems of the North American Indians.

PART I.

Economic Antecedents of Iroquois Culture.

CHAPTER I.—The Environment of the Iroquois.

CHAPTER II.—The Productive Activities of the Iroquois.

CHAPTER III.—THE ORGANIZATION OF PRODUCERS.

CHAPTER IV.—THE WEALTH OF THE IROQUOIS.

CHAPTER V.—The Distribution of Wealth.

CHAPTER VI.—Exchange.

PART II.

Sociological Consequents.

CHAPTER I.—The Family.

CHAPTER II.—State and Government.

CHAPTER III.—Religion.

CHAPTER IV.—Morals.

CHAPTER V.—General Culture.

INTRODUCTION.

The investigations carried on under Professor Keasbey's direction by students of the seminar during the past few years have led to the formulation of certain general conclusions in regard to the development of primitive societies.

An economy, according to Professor Keasbey, may be defined as "a system of activities whereby the potential utilities inherent in the environment are through utilization converted into actual utilities."[1] The motives making for utilization are everywhere the same; nevertheless, since the potential utilities of one environment differ from those of another, processes of utilization must differ accordingly. Starting from this principle, it has been found convenient to plot off the surface of the earth into a series of typical environments; *e. g.* the jungle, the arctic, the barren, the forest, the plain, the desert oasis, the river valley, etc. The nature of the potential utilities characteristic of each of these environments seems in every case to determine the process of utilization and hence the economic life of the inhabitants. Everywhere similar conditions seem to result in similar forms of utilization. Between the economic activities and the social institutions of mankind there is also perceptible a relation of cause and effect. Everywhere like systems of utilization give rise to like familial, political, and ecclesiastical institutions.

The work assigned me has been confined chiefly to the primitive societies of North America. The results gained from an intensive study of Iroquois life, I shall present in this monograph.

In order to make plain the significance of Iroquois institutions it will be advisable, in a general way, to relate their environment with the other environments of North America, and their manner of life with the manners of life of other Indian tribes. At the

[1] "A Classification of Economies." Reprint from *Proc. Am. Philos. Soc.*, Vol. XLI, No. 169, page 1.

beginning of the sixteenth century, North America, exclusive of Mexico, included several more or less distinct cultural areas, which may be enumerated in the following order: first, the *Arctic Environment,* extending all the way across the northern-most zone of the continent, its southern boundary being the indefinite line marking the transition from the frigid to the cold temperate zone; second, the *Barren Environment,* stretching from the Rocky Mountains on the east to the Pacific coast ranges on the west, and from the Columbia River on the north to the Colorado River valley on the south; third, the *Forest Environment,* including the eastern portion of the continent from the Atlantic to the western edge of the forest belt, and also the narrow region lying along the Pacific coast west of the Coast Ranges; fourth, the *Plain Environment,* extending from the edge of the forest belt to the Rocky Mountains; and fifth, the *Desert-Oasis Environment,* stretching from the Colorado River southward to the Gulf and into Mexico. Each of these environments possessed certain characteristic features which determined the manner of life of the early inhabitants.

In the sterile and ice-bound environment of the Arctic area, the basis of subsistence was fish, whales, and seals. Even this food supply was often scanty and difficult to obtain. In general, the conditions under which man carried on the struggle for existence were extremely hard, and allowed very little opportunity for progress.

The western slope of the Rocky Mountains and the great plain adjoining well deserved the epithet "barren." This region, cut off by the coast ranges from the moist breezes of the Pacific and by the Rocky Mountains from the Atlantic winds, was an arid and sterile desert with little or no vegetation and but a scanty supply of fish and small game. Thus the Barren, like the Arctic Environment, offered little encouragement to primitive progress.

The eastern forest region rejoiced in a mild climate and a plentiful rainfall. Before the European settlement the whole district was covered by a forest of varying density, the trees growing thickest in the temperate and warm temperate parts of the east and south, and becoming fewer in the north toward Hudson's Bay, and in the west throughout the park-like region in the vicinity of the Mississippi. The whole section was stocked with fish and game. From the Great Lakes southward, the climate was warm and the soil fertile enough to encourage more or less cultivation of maize in the river valleys and open spaces and clearings in the woods. Generally speaking, it was an environment conducing to a hunting and fishing life, with a growing dependence upon maize culture toward the south.

The western forest environment, stretching from the Columbia River valley down along the Pacific coast, was characterized by an equable oceanic climate and by an abundant flora and fauna. It was especially rich in fish, small game, nuts, roots, etc. The main difference between the western and the eastern forest environment is to be found in the fact that in the latter the main supply was game, while in the former fish took the chief place.

The Great Plain, between the Mississippi River and the Rocky Mountains, though traversed by several large river systems tributary to the Mississippi, was a comparatively arid region with but a scanty rainfall. Hence there was but little vegetation. Nevertheless, this section of the continent was originally well stocked with game. Over its vast extent great herds of buffalo ranged, subsisting on the long succulent grass with which the prairie was covered, and migrating from north to south, and back again, according to the seasons. Before the Discovery the Prairie was not inhabited, except by occasional bands of buffalo hunters on expeditions from their villages on the Mississippi and its great western tributaries. The introduction of the horse gave a decided impetus to buffalo hunting as a means of livelihood. After this event the great stock of the Sioux pushed farther and farther into the wilderness, and developed more and more perfectly the economy in social life typical of nomadic plain-dwelling people the world over.

The region south of the barren plateau, between the Colorado River valley and the Gulf of Mexico, has been called the desert-oasis environment. Here the sterile highland was deeply gashed by swift-flowing rivers, which found their sources in the Rocky Mountains and emptied into the Gulf of California on the one hand, and into the Gulf of Mexico on the other. In the deep river valleys were rich alluvial deposits which, with the help of irrigation, could be, and were, cultivated. Hence the aboriginal inhabitants of the region were gathered in small isolated agricultural communities, depending for subsistence chiefly upon maize culture.

The environmental conditions of each of the areas just described required in every case the adoption by the primitive inhabitants of an economic system suitable to their surroundings. Their economy in turn determined the nature of their social institutions. In fact, the forms of the family, of the state, and of religion among any given people, are, according to the hypothesis, to be regarded as sociological consequents of certain economic antecedents: in other words, they are the outcome of the peculiar systems of production, consumption, and distribution that have proved most advantageous in a given environment. In the barren environment of the great western desert, marked by extremes of temperature and poverty of flora and fauna, the food-quest consisted primarily of root grubbing and acorn gathering, with some fishing, and hunting of small animals. The means of production consisted of such inventions as were needed to procure food; as, for instance, the bow and arrow, the digging stick, and the basket for carrying roots and nuts. The production group in this case was the family; the wife gathering roots and nuts and bringing up the children, while the husband obtained what fish and game he could find and acted as defender of the group. Anything less than this mere sexual association of labor was impossible, if the species was to be preserved. Anything more extensive in the line of coöperation was likewise made impossible by the scantiness of the food supply, and the consequent necessity of dispersion in the smallest possible groups. "The Mountain Snakes," says Schoolcraft, "exist in small detached bodies and single families, and change their locations so widely that they seem to have no particular claim to any portion."[1] Similar circumstances as regards scarcity of food resulted in a similar manner of life during a large part of the year among the Esquimaux of the Arctic region. We are told that "The Esquimaux live in

[1] Schoolcraft, "Hist. Ind. Tribes," I, 224.

the most perfect state of independence of each other,—the youth, as soon as he is able to build a kaiak and to support himself, no longer observes any family ties, but goes where his fancy takes him." Obviously, therefore, the consumption and distribution group must also have been represented by the family: of exchange, there was no question.

From the point of view of politics, also, among the Esquimaux, as among the Indians of the Great Desert, the family was at once the largest and the smallest group. Mere congregation of these units might occur at certain seasons in spots where acorns or fish were plentiful. At the most, however, only a loose temporary organization resulted. The family remained the social unit and wandered off again when it pleased, a complete political and production group. Within the family, husband and wife associated their labor in producing the surplus; nevertheless, the female, isolated from others of her own sex, was entirely dependent upon the male for defense and hence for access to the source of supply. The man, then, may be said to have controlled the social surplus; hence sovereignty belonged to him, and he wielded unlimited authority over the little group of which he was the head: in other words, the rule of the husband and father was the only government known to these domestic economists. The religion and morals of this stage of culture were of the simplest description. Their religion was the lowest form of Fetishism—abject fear of disutilities and reverence of utilities.

A stage above the domestic economists of the Arctic region and the Great Desert stood the village economists of the western forest. True, the latter had made no distinct advance in methods of production nor in political organization; yet from the economic position which they occupied, some progress in these respects became possible. On the northwest coast, the periodical ascent of the rivers by the salmon at the spawning season afforded the aborigines an abundant and regular food supply. Families, therefore, did not need to separate as they increased in numbers; on the contrary, large gentile groups remained together, settled near the good fishing places, while their means of production tended to become preëminently a stock of implements and inventions of especial use in fishing. As a consequence, to the acquisitive goods of the domestic economy were added a new set of commodities; nevertheless there was no material advance in the methods of production. Though the abundance of the food supply rendered possible the congregation of large numbers of families, the nature of the supply called for no great amount of coöperation among producers. In the construction and defense of the fish-weir there was indeed some combination, but this was of the loosest kind. In the main, the family continued to be the unit of production and consumption—the husband attending to the catching of the fish, and the women of the family looking after the other productive activities.[1] The family support was further augmented by slave labor, now made possible by the abundance of the food supply, and also by the fact that the fishing implements supplied to the captive slave could not be used as weapons to attack the master. The fact that slave labor was practicable also caused some slight differences in distribution as between different families. Hence occurred a faint manifestation of the phenomenon of prestige value. Some families were richer than others in slaves, and hence in stores of food, blankets, etc. Furthermore, the more slaves a man had, the more wives he could own, since the surplus product of the slaves' labor could be used to support these women. Slaves therefore came to be regarded as a sort of standard of value, in terms of which a man's wealth was sometimes estimated.

The introduction of the village economy wrought little essential change in the constitution of the state. The village was, in the main, only a congregation of many domestic economies. There might be, of course, some temporary military organization for purposes of defense; undoubtedly, too, some general influence was constantly exerted by one or two of the older and richer men, for the purpose of keeping peace and order among the different families; nevertheless, the political and governmental system differed but little from that of domestic economists. Each family or gens in the village continued to form a separate political and governmental unit, in which the father or patriarch was the sovereign power.

[1] Keasbey, "Inst. of Society," *Internat. Mo.*, I, 383, 386.

So far but one really fundamental type of economy has appeared. This is the "domestic" system, adapted to regions where the nature of the food-supply makes coöperation not advantageous. Even the village economy was a mere aggregation of domestic economies. Yet a distinction must be made between the village and the domestic systems, because in the former the occasional appearance of a new principle is noticeable. The management of the weir in the salmon fishing season and the defense of their collective riparian rights caused at certain seasons the formation of an organization among the men of the different families. This temporary union of the men of the village into a band, each member of which coöperated with all the rest in order to carry out certain definite purposes, was the clan: hence, for the time being, the family as a productive and political unit disappeared, and the clan took its place.

Where the coöperative method of production had through force of environmental circumstances reached a fuller development and become comparatively permanent, the general character of village life was correspondingly altered. The settlement was no longer a mere aggregation of families each economically and politically independent of the others. On the contrary, its chief productive activities were carried on by an association of coöperating individuals, bound together not merely by family affection, but by the ties of economic interest. In order to keep up the population, the family remained in existence, but it had no economic function beyond that of consumption. As a productive association, it had become merged in the clan; and political sovereignty passed from the individual fathers of families to the clan as a whole. The latter now controlled the access to the source of supply, and consequently had absolute power over such of the inhabitants of the village as were without the limits of the clan, and were dependent upon it for support or defense. Government, therefore, was representative only of the clan. In the establishment of this clan principle is to be found the origin of organized society. "The clan," says Professor Keasbey, "is neither a confederacy of domestic units nor an aggregation of individuals, but an organization in the full force of the term—it is a corporation, an economic body politic, whose constituent members are not so much severally bound, as jointly united in a common cause. The permanent productive clan is, in short, the first form of the state."[1]

The first stage of development of the clan economy occurred in the Plain environment. In this region, the buffalo supplied all the prime necessaries of existence. The wandering habits of the animal and its gregarious tendencies taken together with the nature of its habitat had a distinct effect upon the economy of the human beings who depended upon it for subsistence. The buffalo hunting tribes were naturally clan economists. After the introduction of the horse had enabled tribes like the Dacotahs and Comanches to push out farther into the Plain, and to depend entirely upon the buffalo as their source of supply, the process of organization seems to have been completed.[2] Production ceased to be carried on by the family group with its mere sexual association of labor. On the contrary, the productive unit was a group outside the family and even antagonistic to it. Withdrawing from their families all the able-bodied men, it united them, under a leader with authority of life and death, in a closely organized coöperative band. Each member of the group had his part to perform in the buffalo hunt, some acted as scouts, others as a sort of police, others as simple marksmen.[3] A similarly rigid military organization existed. Just as every able-bodied man was a hunter, so also was he a warrior, likely at any time to be called by force of public opinion to join some war party, and under the leadership of a war chief to coöperate with others in the defense of the hunting grounds or in the preservation of their prestige among their neighbors. To this hunting and warring republican clan, the women of the group formed a sort of subsidiary and unorganized set of assistants. The means of subsistence once procured by the men's clan, the women prepared it for use. They cut up the meat, and prepared the skins for use as clothing and

[1] "Inst. of Soc.," *Internat. Mo.*, I, p. 395.

[2] Schoolcraft, "Hist. Ind. Tribes," I, 207–208; IV, 60.
Margry, VI, 444–445.
Perrot, pp. 60–64.

[3] Dodge, "The Plains of the Great West," pp. 263–266.

tent coverings.[1] Besides doing this work, they gathered roots, and in some cases cultivated a little maize. Their labor, however, was not of the sort that either requires or encourages coöperation: hence they worked individually, without any particular organization among themselves, each producing as the servant of some member of the men's clan; in short, an organized band of men formed the typical production group of the Plains tribes. It controlled the access to the source of supply, and directed the labor of the women. Though the consumption group was still the family, the unit of distribution was the clan. In the latter, each member received a share of the animals killed in the hunt, the actual slayers receiving some special portion as a mark of their prowess.[2]

The sociological effects of the republican clan economy are evident, in the first place, in the family. Paternal authority was supreme in the lodge. Wife and children belonged absolutely to the husband and father, and all purely family affairs were regulated by him, without reference to any outside organization.[3] Men who could procure several wives did so, since they were useful as laborers and child-bearers. Sons were valued as adding to the wealth of the family while they remained unmarried, and as always increasing the influence of the father. Daughters, on the other hand, were regarded merely as articles to be sold to the highest bidder. In all this, conditions did not differ greatly from those prevalent in the domestic and village economies.

Politically, however, there arose a new state of affairs. The state was now identical with the male clan—the latter controlling the sources of the surplus, and so possessing sovereign power in political life. To the women belonged no shadow of sovereignty. Speaking of the Comanches, Schoolcraft says, "Females have no voice or even influence in their councils,"[4] and are "held in small

[1] Schoolcraft, "Hist. Ind. Tribes," I, 236; II, 132.

[2] Schoolcraft, "Hist. Ind. Tribes," II, 185.

[3] Schoolcraft, "Hist. Ind. Tribes," II, 131-132—"A husband exercises unbounded authority over the person of his wife."

Bancroft, I, 509—"Every father holds undisputed sway over his children."

[4] Schoolcraft, "Hist. Ind. Tribes," II, 131.

estimation."[1] Hence, from the women's point of view, the government was an absolute despotism. Within the clan, on the other hand, the purest republicanism prevailed, all good hunters and warriors having an equal share in the management of affairs.[2] The chieftanship was given to the ablest and most experienced hunter, especially if he had a large number of blood relations to support his claims. He exercised governmental powers, however, only as the representative of the sovereign body of hunters and warriors, and with their advice and consent. All decisions of importance were made by the clan council, the voice of the majority prevailing.

In the Desert-Oasis environment, south of the Colorado River the clan principle manifested itself in a still more developed form. The inhabitants of this region depended for subsistence mainly upon maize culture. In this industry women were the pioneers. Hence in the course of time they formed a productive association of their own which, in certain circumstances, came to compete with the men's hunting and war clan, and gained the first place in the economic life of the community. Eventually, when conditions required, as among the Pueblo Indians, the men also took up agriculture; and the two clans united in one body. This communal clan, composed of both men and women, was the form of organization characteristic of the primitive agricultural settlements of the southwest. The distribution group was now the communal clan, though the family still continued to be the unit of consumption. The family, however, showed the effect of economic antecedents in the reduced authority of the father and the correspondingly increased influence of the mother. The wife rather than the husband was now regarded as the head of the family. The state, too, showed the influence of the changed methods of production. Sovereignty resided in the body of co-operating producers that controlled the sources of the surplus; *i. e.* in the communal clan. Women became sharers in the possession of sovereign power. Government was carried on by purely

[1] Schoolcraft, "Hist. Ind. Tribes," I, 235.

[2] *Ibid.*, V, 687; II, 130.

democratic methods, all having a voice in the management of affairs. Age and experience and consequent knowledge of climatic conditions affecting agricultural operations were the qualifications sought for in those who were chosen governors of the community.

The Plains and the Oases of the Desert presented, perhaps, the clearest examples of each form of clan economy when isolated and complete in its development. The Eastern Forest environment, however, affords the student the best opportunity to observe the slow growth of the coöperative principle. Within its limits, from north to south, were economies in every stage of development. In the cold and thickly wooded section about the St. Lawrence River, where the food supply was comparatively scarce and irregular, the domestic economy prevailed for the greater part of the year. Congregation occurred in spots where food was temporarily abundant, but when the season was over each family wandered off by itself, to carry on its food-quest as best it might. The Quebec Indians, for instance, were "wanderers . . . during the six winter months—roving here and there according as they might find game, two or three families erecting their cabins together in one place, two or three in another, and so on."[1] In times of famine, "they play, so to speak, at 'save himself who can'—deserting each other and abandoning all interest in the common welfare, each one strives to find something for himself. Then the children, women, and for that matter all those who cannot hunt, die of cold and hunger."[2] Thus in times of comparative plenty the village system might appear for a season, while in times of great scarcity the food-quest became a purely individual matter. In general, however, the economy characteristic of the northern portion of the Eastern Forest environment was domestic. In the warmer climate and more favorable conditions of the central portion, the principles of association and coöperation began to operate. Here two clans—the men's and

[1] Jes. Rel. IV, 203. Cf. "La Potherie," I, 118 sq.; "Le Clercq," 67 sq. "Lettres Edifiantes," X, 315 sq. Jes. Rel. II, 77; LXII, 221; XXXIII, 153.

[2] Jes. Rel. VII, 49.

the women's, the one a warring and hunting, and the other an agricultural organization—existed side by side in the same community. Finally, in the warm districts of the far South, there was developed the regular communal clan economy, typical of the primitive agricultural community. Among the Ayennis, near the mouth of the Mississippi River, says Charlevoix, "when the season for cultivation arrives, there assemble sometimes as many as a hundred persons, the men and the women separately. They work thus until they have cultivated a certain portion of ground, the owner of which subsequently feasts the workers. . . . The next day they begin again, and this goes on until all the fields are worked over."[1] Among the Natchez, progress had gone so far that the men of the community really did most of the work. A desirable husband, according to the Jesuit Relation, had to be "a skilful hunter, a good warrior, and an excellent field-worker."[2]

[1] Charlevoix, II, 15–16.

[2] Jes. Rel. LXVIII, 141. Cf. Carr, "Mounds," Sm. Inst. Rep., 1891, pp. 524 note, 527, 530.

Lafitau, II, 80; "Lettres Edifiantes," XX, 118–119.

PART I.

CHAPTER I.

THE ENVIRONMENT OF THE IROQUOIS.

The Iroquois tribes inhabited the central portion of the eastern forest region of North America. Here, in an environment transitional between that of the upper and that of the lower sections of the area in question, they developed a culture which is likewise to be regarded as a connecting link between those which prevailed to the north and to the south of them. Iroquois civilization stood midway between the lowest and the highest stage of the natural state. An analysis of the life of these tribes, therefore, affords an admirable demonstration of the laws according to which society was first developed.

Though the history of the Iroquois before the coming of the Europeans is mainly a matter of tradition and conjecture, yet the present consensus of opinion is somewhat as follows.[1] The valleys drained by the Columbia River and the streams flowing into Puget Sound were probably the early home of the Iroquois. Here, not less than ten centuries ago, they lived as a fish-eating people, ignorant of agriculture and organized only to the extent generally characteristic of the village economy of the northwest coast. Migrating from this region, they finally reached the Mississippi Valley, where they learned agriculture. Here the Cherokees broke off from the main stem and turned southwards. The other tribes, including the ancestors of the Hurons, Eries, and Neutrals, as well as those of the Five Nations, remained together for a longer period, settled probably in the Ohio Valley.[2] From

[1] Morgan, "League" (ed. 1901), Appendix B.
Thwaites, Jes. Rel. VIII, 293.

[2] Mr. Morgan's theory that the first sedentary home of the Iroquois was in the vicinity of Montreal, is altogether improbable. At any rate,

here, the different tribes of the Iroquois stock scattered to their historic locations in Virginia, Pennsylvania, New York and Canada. At the time of their first acquaintance with the Europeans, the Iroquois and Hurons had long been settled in their respective homes. The country of the Iroquois in the seventeenth century lay south of Lake Ontario between the Hudson River and Lake Erie. In the center of this tract, occupying the Onondaga River valley and the adjacent hills, was the tribe of the Onondagas. On their right hand, around and near Oneida Lake, were the principal villages of the Oneidas. On their left, along the east shore of Cayuga Lake and the ridge to the eastward, the Cayugas were settled. The western frontier, as far as the Genesee River, was occupied by the Senecas, while the eastern boundaries were defended by the Mohawks, who lived in the valley of the river bearing their name.

From the point of view of geographic unity, the location finally chosen by the Iroquois was well adapted to be the permanent habitat of tribes already connected by ties of kinship and association. The region was enclosed on the north and west by the St. Lawrence River and by Lakes Ontario and Erie, while on the east it was shut in by the Appalachian mountain ranges. Within these boundaries there were no bars to communication or differences in environment. Hence the tribes living in the region would naturally tend to develop along similar lines, and become more closely united among themselves. Although the Iroquois were protected by mountain and lake barriers from outside attack, nevertheless they were not entirely imprisoned. Situated on the highest part of the region east of the Mississippi, they had the best possible highways leading into the outer world in the great

he is undoubtedly mistaken in his idea, based upon some vague tradition, that the Iroquois learned agriculture from the Adirondacks. The Valley of the St. Lawrence, where maize crops often failed, was not an environment where agriculture was likely to be adopted by a people hitherto ignorant of it. Furthermore, even though it might have been here that they first learned to cultivate maize, it is absurd to suppose that the Adirondacks were their teachers, since the latter were nomad hunters who knew nothing about agriculture. Cf. Lloyd in Morgan's League. Ed. 1901, Appendix B.

rivers whose headwaters find their sources here. These were routes whose swift currents made an easy exit for Iroquois warriors and a difficult approach for hostile bands. In short, says Mr. Morgan, the Iroquois, "situated upon the head waters of the Hudson, the Delaware, the Susquehanna, the Ohio, and the St. Lawrence rivers—flowing in every direction to the sea—held within their jurisdiction the gates of the country, and could through them descend at will upon any point."[1]

The Iroquois territory itself was, in general, hilly and covered with forests of hemlock, maple, pine, oak, and other trees characteristic of the temperate zone. Among the hills, however, were many fertile valleys, and here and there were open tracts of alluvial land,—all favorable to such agriculture as the inhabitants knew how to carry on. Onondaga, for example, was a hilly district, but, says one of the early travellers, "there is a small valley, which is very fertile, and yields almost incredible crops of corn, which is plentiful about here."[2] One of the Jesuits, writing to his superior from his station among the Cayugas, says, "Goiogouen is the fairest country that I have seen in America. . . . It is a tract situated between two lakes and not exceeding four leagues in width, consisting of almost uninterrupted plains, the woods bordering which are extremely beautiful."[3] In the Seneca country, there were several such open tracts, formed by a recession of the hills from the bed of the Genesee River. In one place "the alluvial flats through which the river meanders for four or five miles above, and as many miles below, are from one to two miles wide . . . level . . . and fertile. . . . These flats are encompassed on each side by a rolling country, gradually rising as it recedes from the river. . . . This was the terrestrial paradise of the Senecas."[4]

So far as its water supply was concerned, the Iroquois country was extremely well off. It was intersected by innumerable streams and dotted with lakes ranging in size from small ponds to large sheets of water several miles in extent. Of the larger

[1] Morgan, "League" (ed. 1901), I, 38.
[2] Schoolcraft, "Hist. Ind. Tribes," IV, 340.
[3] Jes. Rel. LVI, 49.
[4] "Life of Mary Jemison," pp. 85 sq.

lakes, there were about a half dozen distributed throughout the different cantons of the Five Nations. In the middle of the Seneca country was Canandaigua Lake, and east of it was Seneca Lake; the Cayuga territory contained Cayuga Lake, a sheet of water twenty-eight miles long and from two to four miles wide; the Onondagas owned Skaneateles Lake; the Oneidas controlled the lake named after them; and the Mohawk country rejoiced in numberless lakes, including Lake Champlain and Lake George on its eastern borders. Throughout the whole country, springs were frequent; and the variety in the kinds of waters they gave was great, ranging from the clearest drinking water to the salt springs and the mineral springs for which the region is now famous. All these bodies of water—streams, lakes and springs—formed centers of animal and vegetable life, while as routes for internal travel the rivers and lakes were invaluable.

Climatic conditions were, also, not unpropitious. In this region there was a regular succession of seasons—spring and summer, autumn and winter. The summer was long and warm enough to have encouraged aboriginal maize-culture, while the winters were not so severe as in the region north of the Great Lakes. The rainfall was abundant, and the soil, especially on the river-flats and in other open or cleared spots, was by nature extremely fertile.

The environment of the Iroquois was, therefore, comparatively rich in potential utilities. Animal and vegetable food products were abundant. Moose and deer, bear and beaver, and many other smaller animals furnished a plentiful supply of meat, while the stock of fish was practically inexhaustible. In 1655, we hear of the Salmon River, northeast of Oswego;—" such is the richness of this stream that it yields at all seasons various kinds of fish. In the spring, as soon as the snows melt, it is full of gold-colored fish; next come carp, and finally the achigen (black bass). . . . Then comes the brill, and at the end of May . . . sturgeon are killed . . . . All the rest of the year until winter, salmon furnishes food . . . ."[1] At Onondaga Lake, says a Jesuit mis-

[1] Jes. Rel. XLII, 71; Cf. Jes. Rel., XLIII, 261.

sionary, "besides the fish caught at different seasons, eels are so abundant in the summer that a man can harpoon as many as one thousand in one night."[1] Multitudinous also were the birds that in spring flocked to the lakes and ponds of the Iroquois country. Nearly all of them were more or less suitable for food. Among them were cranes, pelicans, wild swans, ducks, geese and turkeys, pigeons, turtle doves, gulls, and loons. Near Seneca Lake, for instance, swans and bustards were abundant all through the winter, while in spring clouds of all sorts of wild fowl arrived from the South. "As to Onondaga Lake," says the Jesuit chronicler, "turtle doves from all the country around flock thither toward spring, in so great numbers that they are caught in nets."[2]

A glance at the vegetable life of the Iroquois territory shows a correspondingly plentiful food-supply. The cultivated plants—maize, beans, squashes and melons—the Iroquois had brought with them from the Mississippi Valley. To these bases of subsistence, the nuts, roots, and fruits indigenous to the region formed a welcome adjunct. Nut-bearing trees—the hickory, pig-nut, butternut, chestnut, walnut and oak—were numerous. The sugar maple also supplied an important article of food in the syrup which was made from its sap. Edible and medicinal roots were also abundant. Among the fruit and berry products were wild raspberries, whortle-berries, strawberries, and cranberries. Wild grapes, sweet enough to be agreeable to the taste, grew in spots, where forest fires had occurred. The may-apple, the crab-apple, the paw-paw, and other wild fruits completed the list.[3]

In fine, the food utilities of the Iroquois country were numerous and valuable. Wild animals, especially deer, were plentiful, as were also many varieties of fish and birds. Cultivated plants, such as maize, beans and squashes flourished; and of nuts, fruits and roots, there was no scarcity.

Products available as raw materials were no less abundant than those useful as food. The skin of the deer, the bear, and the

[1] Jes. Rel. XLII, 95.
[2] Jes. Rel. XLII, 95.
[3] Loskiel, pp. 68 sq. Jes. Rel. XLIII, 257; XXVIII, 111.

beaver, as well as those of smaller animals, provided all needed articles of clothing and most of the other coverings used by the Iroquois, while bones and sinews furnished material for various implements. Shells of mollusks formed a source of supply for tools and utensils. The Iroquois were also able to draw to a great extent upon the vegetable world for raw materials. The wood and bark of the forest trees offered a suitable and convenient supply of material for their dwellings, and for many of their implements and utensils; thus, ash, elm, fir, spruce, and cedar bark were all available as coverings for the wooden frames of their houses; the wood of the white ash covered with the bark of the red elm made good canoes;[1] and hickory wood was a useful material in the manufacture of snow shoes. From the vegetable kingdom came also several products employed in the textile industry of the aborigines. Wild vines furnished ready-made ropes and cables. The fiber from the inner bark of the slippery elm and other trees, and also of the *Dirca palustris* or moosewood, a little shrub growing on the hillsides, offered a good material for the manufacture of cords and coarse threads. The wild hemp plant (*Apocynum cannabinum*) was useful for the same purpose. Among the products of value in the manufacture of textiles were the reeds and cornhusks of which mats and other articles could be woven. Finally, there were several plants whose juices were useful as dyes.

The mineral resources of their environment contained but few utilities for the Iroquois. Because of his ignorance of the art of smelting, copper, which could be hammered out cold, was about the only metal of use to the American Indian; of this, there was very little to be found in New York, while access to the Lake Superior mines was cut off by intervening hostile tribes; hence, before the coming of the Europeans, the Iroquois had no metal instruments.[2] Stone and clay suitable for pottery existed in considerable quantities in their country. The clay they utilized in the manufacture of their earthenware vessels, and of the local

[1] Not as good as the birch bark of the Northern Forest, however.

[2] Beauchamp, N. Y. St. Mus. Bul., No. 55. "Metallic Instruments of the N. Y. Indians."

horn-stone they made a few of their ruder articles. In general, however, they used stone much less than wood. The reasons are not difficult to conjecture. In the first place, since they had no metal instruments, they would naturally prefer to utilize the softer and more easily worked material; in the second place, supplies of wood were undoubtedly more accessible than stone would be for a relatively sedentary, semi-agricultural people like the Iroquois. Available stone would be hard to find, especially since the village would naturally avoid a stony site. On the other hand, land had to be cleared and wood cut in order to prepare the maize fields and procure fuel. Hence, the material for the manufacture of wooden articles was provided without extra trouble. Everything considered, it is not hard to understand why the Iroquois utilized wood as a raw material, rather than stone.

To sum up;—the home-country of the Iroquois may be described as a forest region, stocked with an abundant supply of wild animals, fish, nuts, fruits, and roots; at the same time, it was a country of temperate climate, well-watered and fertile, with many open spaces suitable for maize-culture; hence it was an environment favorable to the development of a hunting and fishing and semi-agricultural life.

Similar features marked the environment of the cognate tribe of the Hurons. Their territory, the peninsula between Lake Huron and Lakes Erie and Ontario, was somewhat more open and suitable for agriculture than that of the Iroquois, and although the supply of game was scantier; yet, on the other hand, there was even a greater abundance of fish than among the Iroquois. Hence the Hurons would naturally devote themselves somewhat more to maize-culture and fishing, and less to hunting, than was the case among the Iroquois. In spite of such minor differences, however, the general similiarity between the previous history and the final environment of both Hurons and Iroquois justifies us in regarding them as essentially one people.[1]

[1] Jes. Rel. VIII, 115; XV, 153; X, 103; LIV, 151; XIII, n. 17, p. 255.

CHAPTER II.

The Productive Activities of the Iroquois.

The main productive activities of the Iroquois were nut and fruit gathering, root grubbing, trapping, hunting, fishing, and agriculture. From the earliest days of their life in the Far West, they had depended upon fish and game, and upon the nuts and fruits to be found in their environment; with maize they became acquainted in their journey across the continent; and in the favorable environment of the Eastern Forest, they gained support from all these sources.

The food supply upon which primitive domestic economists chiefly depend was not neglected by the Iroquois. Root-grubbing and nut and fruit gathering were a regular part of their yearly labor. The Senecas, for instance, depended to a considerable extent upon the nut crop. In 1669, writes one of the Jesuit fathers, an abundant harvest caused so great joy among them that " one sees everywhere only games, dances, and feasts."[1] Maple sugar making, also, was an important annual event, celebrated with feasting.[2]

These lines of production, however, were distinctly subsidiary to the serious business of hunting and trapping, inasmuch as the Iroquois, for a great part of their subsistence, depended upon the useful animals and birds of their immediate environment, and even far outside of their own boundaries. The chief animals of the chase were the deer and the bear; wild fowl and several varieties of small game, such as otters, martens, hares, and squirrels, were also hunted. The value of the beaver to the Iroquois hunter dates largely from the time of the coming of the Europeans and the beginning of the fur-trade; before that time,

[1] Jes. Rel. LIV, 97; cf. La Potherie, III, 20; Jes. Rel. LII, 23.

[2] Morgan, "League" (ed. 1901), II, 251; Lafitau, III, 140.

the beaver was not so highly appreciated.[1] The hunting season was confined mainly to the winter months. During the rest of the year only desultory trapping was done. The fall and spring were the seasons for the capture of wild fowl; from January to May, during the hibernating period, was the best time for hunting bears; while the deer and beaver hunt was mainly an affair of the first four months of winter.[2] From October until January, parties small and large scattered in all directions in search of the desired game. Seneca expeditions went to Niagara for the beaver hunt, or southward to the Chemung River for deer and other game. They also penetrated by way of the Alleghany into Ohio, a favorite hunting ground of all the Iroquois. The Cayugas found a wealth of game in the valley of the Susquehanna, in fact, all over Pennsylvania. They, with bands from the other Iroquois tribes, often roamed as far south as the Potomac in search of deer and bear. Onondaga parties also frequented the Susquehanna region, descending thither by way of the Chemung River. Other bands, turning northward, went into Canada. The Oneidas descended the Unadilla, or went north into the region watered by the Black River. The Mohawks hunted in the Adirondacks, or near the head waters of the Delaware and Susquehanna.[3] About midwinter, all these scattered groups came back to their homes, bringing with them the supplies of meat left over from the winter's consumption. After this there was little regular work until with the spring came the beginning of the fishing season.

As hunting was a winter occupation, so fishing formed one of the main activities of the summer months. From the middle of March until the beginning of winter and the deer-hunting season, fishing of one kind or another was always going on. The varieties of fish taken were many, ranging from the fresh water clam[4] up to sturgeon large enough to be killed with a hatchet. The salmon and eel fisheries were the most productive. The former

[1] Beauchamp, "Iroquois Trail," p. 91.
[2] Loskiel, p. 80.
[3] Morgan, "League," 346.
[4] Beauchamp, N. Y. St. Mus. Bul., No. 41, p. 462.

furnished food to the village of Onondaga throughout the summer. Eels, too, were caught during the whole season. Fishing was even more extensively carried on by the Hurons than by the Five Nations, the former doing more or less of it all through the year.[1]

Besides hunting and fishing, the Iroquois carried on another and more developed form of activity, namely, agriculture. Forest hunting, as a rule, demanded little other exertion than that immediately expended in the pursuit and slaughter of the game; agriculture, on the other hand, involved a much longer and more complicated series of operations. The maize upon which the Iroquois largely depended was, on account of the great size of the plant and of its grain, as well as its large returns, the most suitable of all cereals for cultivation by slightly advanced peoples;[2] nevertheless, the labor necessitated by maize culture called for a greater amount of patience and forethought, and meant a higher degree of economic development, than was possible among a people depending for subsistence solely upon forest hunting and fishing. The production of one crop of maize involved four principal stages of procedure,—clearing the ground, planting, cultivating, and harvesting. From beginning to end, the process was the work of a whole summer. Perhaps, if the task of clearing were especially difficult, the first crop taken from a field might be the product of several years' labor. In the open places along the streams the question of clearing did not have to be taken into account.[3] These sites were consequently much sought after. But the necessity of choosing a place comparatively easy to defend against hostile attacks, and other reasons, often compelled the selection of a heavily wooded spot as the site for a village. In such a case, the deforesting of land for cornfields was sometimes a matter of years.[4] Furthermore, the ex-

[1] Jes. Rel. XLIII, 261; XLII, 73; XXXIX, 215; LIV, 151.

[2] Payne, "History of America," I, 354 sq.

[3] Ga-o-sai-gao, for instance, an important Seneca Village, was situated in the middle of an opening of about 2,000 acres, on Honeoye Creek. Morgan, "League" (ed. 1901), II, 210; cf. Beauchamp, N. Y. St. Mus. Bul., No. 32, p. 29.

[4] Lafitau, II, 109; Greenhalgh, Doc. Hist. N. Y., I, 12.

tensive agricultural methods of the Iroquois and the consequent frequent migrations of the village necessitated the repetition of the task of clearing about every ten or twelve years.[1] The ground once cleared, the planting followed. Maize, beans, pumpkins, and melons were the chief crops. The first two were sown in the same field, the stalks of the maize serving as supports for the bean vines. Pumpkins and melons were cultivated in gardens by themselves. Sunflowers and tobacco were also grown to a limited extent. Throughout the summer, careful cultivation of these crops was kept up until finally, amid rejoicing and festivity, the harvest was gathered in and the agricultural labors of the year were ended. Maize culture involved more prolonged and systematic effort than deer-hunting could possibly demand; consequently, maize-culture developed a more advanced manner of life than was to be found in the case of purely hunting tribes: hence, among a people like the Iroquois, where both manners of production existed, there was more or less conflict between agricultural and hunting ideals. Eventually the relative importance of the two as a means of assuring the economic welfare of the community decided the outcome of the struggle.

While there is no doubt that hunting and fishing occupied a position subordinate to agriculture in the Iroquois' economic system, it would certainly be a mistake to imagine that the former pursuits were of slight importance in the life of these tribes. Although the scarcity of game in the Huron territories caused the Hurons to do but little hunting,[2] the activities of the Iroquois in this direction were very considerable. Among the Oneidas hunting was so productive an occupation that, according to the Jesuit Relation, "the fate of the women depends upon their husbands, who supply them with food, and clothes."[3] With both the Hurons and Iroquois, fishing formed no small part of the year's labor. At certain seasons whole communities would abandon their houses and go fishing, sometimes remaining away for

[1] Jes. Rel. XV, 153.

[2] Jes. Rel., XXXVIII, 245.—"The Hurons . . . hunt only for pleasure or on extraordinary occasions."

[3] Jes. Rel., LVII, 123.

weeks. The Jesuit Relation speaks of a camp, "where there were about four hundred savages who had erected their cabins there for fishing."[1] In another Relation, an instance is given where "the scarcity of seasoning for giving some taste to the Turkish wheat boiled in water obliges a large part of the villagers to go in quest of fish at a place ten leagues from here."[2] Evidently, the Iroquois and Hurons depended to a considerable extent for subsistence upon the products of their hunting and fishing.

Nevertheless, it seems certain that for the greater part of their food supply they looked to their maize fields. The exact extent of this dependence as over against that placed upon hunting and fishing, differed with the locality in which each group found itself. It was greater among the Hurons than among the Iroquois, and among the Cayugas than the Senecas—the more agricultural people in each case living in the less densely forested environment.[3]

In general we may conclude that maize rather than meat, had come, in the course of time, to be the chief basis of subsistence of all the Iroquois tribes. The comparatively permanent nature of their villages, and the sites chosen for them, as well as the amount of cultivated land around or near them, are sufficient proof of the statement. The village, as we have seen, was not moved oftener than once in a dozen or more years, and during that time a part of the inhabitants was generally to be found in residence there. Others might go on the periodical hunting and fishing expeditions, and the warriors when engaged in some distant raid might be absent for years at a time; never-

[1] Jes. Rel., XXVI, 41.

[2] Jes. Rel., LIII, 243; cf. Jes. Rel., XV, 113, 125; XIX, 87; LIV, 151; LII, 175; LIV, 81.

[3] Hiawatha at the formation of the confederacy says in addressing the different tribes:—"And you (the Cayugas) the people who live in the open country, and possess much wisdom, shall be the fifth nation, because you understand better the art of raising corn and beans, and making houses." But to the Senecas he says, "You, whose dwelling is in the dark forest, and whose home is everywhere, shall be the fourth nation, because of your superior cunning in hunting." Schoolcraft, "Hist. Ind. Tribes," III, 317.

theless, all regarded the home village as their permanent headquarters, and returned to it when the expedition was over. Not only the permanence of the settlements, but also their situation, is evidence of the agricultural bent of their inhabitants. In choosing a site, the Iroquois looked primarily for a spot favorable to agriculture. Naturally, any site chosen must not be too much exposed to attack by hostile war parties; but, "in any event, due regard was had to the soil. . . . fishing and hunting advantages determined their camps, but their towns had regard to the culture of the fields. A fertile soil, easily worked, but in a secure situation, was one of the first requisites. Of course water must always be near."[1] The amount of land cultivated relative to the size of the town is, again, proof that the Iroquois were becoming an agricultural rather than a hunting people. A village field often extended over an area of several hundred acres, in which enough corn was raised in one season to support the whole population, and to lay aside a large surplus. Greenhalgh says that in 1677 Onondaga had cornfields extending for two miles on each side of the town. Besides feeding herself, she had enough to supply her neighbors, the Oneidas, who had moved into a new location and were not yet able to prepare all the land they needed.[2] Of all the other towns, Greenhalgh's invariable assertion is that "they have abundance of Corne." The extent of cultivation may be estimated from the great quantities of corn destroyed by the French and American expeditions against the Iroquois. The former in 1687 destroyed four Seneca villages, and consumed nearly a week in cutting down the adjacent fields of corn. Even then the Senecas were not left to starve; for the other Iroquois nations were well able to supply them from their surplus.[3] The Hurons were even more agricultural in habit

[1] Beauchamp, N. Y. St. Mus. Bul., No. 32, p. 23.

[2] Greenhalgh, Doc. Hist. N. Y., I, 12.—"Onondaga is situate upon a hill that is very large, the banke on each side extending itself at least two miles, all cleared land, whereon the corne is planted. . . . They plant abundance of corne, which they sell to the Onyades. The Onondagas are said to be about three hundred and fifty fighting men."

[3] Carr, "Mounds," Sm. Inst. Rep., 1891, pp. 513 sq.

than the Iroquois. The former cultivated corn in such quantities that they were able to store up a surplus large enough to support them for three or four years, and to exchange for skins with the wild hunting tribes of the north. Corn was, in fact, " the chief of their riches."[1]

From the standpoint of their productive activities, then, the Iroquois may be said to have been upon a transitional stage, corresponding to the nature of their environment. In their hunting life they resembled the tribes of the northern forest; in so far as they depended for subsistence upon maize culture, their manner of production resembled that of the nations far to the south of them; in the process of evolution from the hunting to the agricultural manner of production, however, they had gone more than half way.

Besides the primary productive activities of which we have been speaking, the Iroquois naturally carried on a certain amount of manufacturing. During the time of comparative leisure toward the end of the winter, many of the raw materials produced during the hunting season were worked up into finished articles. Other materials, procured at various times, were also made into commodities of different sorts; thus, skins were shaped into garments and coverings, wood and bark were cut and prepared for use in various ways, textiles were woven out of bark and hemp fiber, and earthenware vessels were molded. All these processes will be spoken of in detail in a subsequent section.

[1] Carr, "Mounds," Sm. Inst. Rep., 1891, p. 514; Jes. Rel. XXIX, 247—"The Indian corn which is the chief of their riches."

CHAPTER III.

Organization of Producers.

Two distinct sorts of production prevailed among the Iroquois. On the one hand, were grouped root grubbing, nut and fruit gathering, trapping, hunting, and fishing; on the other hand, stood agriculture. The former activities ordinarily result in the domestic or village economy, with only an occasional appearance of the men's clan: the latter lead to a sedentary life, entirely governed by the clan principle. What, then, was the effect of these conflicting conditions upon the economic methods of the Iroquois? In other words, who were the producers; into what classes were they divided; what was the internal organization of each class; and finally, which class, all things considered, occupied the position of greatest importance in the economic life of the Iroquois?

It seems almost unnecessary to say that the whole population, men and women, had a share in production. Neither hunting, fishing, nor agriculture, as it was carried on by the Iroquois, allowed the permanent appropriation of the sources of supply by any individual or group to the detriment of any others who were able and willing to work. Consequently, no one could live exclusively on the product of another's labor, and all must exert themselves to make their own living.

There was, nevertheless, among the Iroquois, as among all primitive peoples, a sexual division of labor—that is to say, certain lines of production were pursued chiefly or entirely by the men; others by the women of the community. The Iroquois men occupied themselves mainly in hunting, fishing, trading, and making war; the women devoted themselves to agriculture, nut, fruit, and root gathering, and housekeeping: the work of manufacturing the means of production and articles of consumption, the men and women divided pretty evenly between them. "The part of the men," says the Jesuit Relation of 1652–3, "is only war, hunting, fishing, trade in various countries and the preparation of the things thereto necessary; as, offensive and defensive weapons, boats, oars and snowshoes."[1] The men, furthermore, seem to have made most of the instruments of production; for besides their own implements and weapons, they also made the agricultural tools used by the women.[2] It was their duty, also, to mark out and clear the site for the village,[3] and to do all the heavy work involved in building the houses and the palisade. In addition, the men made no small part of the other finished articles of consumption usually found in an Iroquois village. It was their business to cut all the larger-sized firewood,[4] to make the large bark barrels and boxes used for keeping stores of food, and the wooden plates and spoons needed in the household.[5] Just how much they helped in agriculture is hard to determine. Mr. Carr says that among the Hurons "the men not only habitually cleared the ground—no small undertaking in a heavily timbered region—but they frequently took part in what is technically known as working the crop, and also aided in the labors of the harvest field. This may not have been a part of their duty, but we have the authority of Charlevoix for saying that when asked to aid in gathering the crop, they did not scorn to lend a helping hand."[6] Among the Iroquois the men did decidedly less agricultural work than among the Hurons; but even here evidence goes to show that they cleared the fields and burnt them over in preparation for the sowing.[7] La Potherie

[1] Jes. Rel. XXXVIII, 255.

[2] Sagard, 259; Jes. Rel. XIII, 265; XXIII, 55.

La Potherie, III, 18–19—"L'homme fait des instruments de labourage qui sont de bois."

[3] Lafitau, II, 109—"Ce sont les hommes par toute l'Amèrique qui sont chargés de marquer les champs, et d'en abbatre les gros arbres."

La Potherie, III, 18–19—"Dans les champs l'homme abat les arbres, et les ébranle. L'emploi de l'homme dans le bois l'hiver est de faire la cabane."

[4] Lafitau, II, 109.

[5] Boucher, "Histoire Veritable," p. 101.

[6] Carr, "Mounds," Sm. Inst. Rep., 1891, p. 512.

Cf. Perrot, pp. 106, 181; Jes. Rel., XV, 79; XXXVII, 115.

[7] La Potherie, III, 18—"C'est aux hommes à brûler les champs . . . et ils brûlent les racines des herbes pour semer ensuite."

says that " it is the men's business to burn over the fields." He tells us, too, that they fenced in the gardens and prepared the bundles of corn for drying. In regard to the latter part of this statement, Lafitau supports him.[1] Any further help, the men of the Five Nations, always occupied with war and with hunting, do not seem to have offered to their women.[2] It should be noted, however, that no matter how much or how little the Iroquois or Huron warrior worked in the field, he always acted merely as an assistant, and not as a director or owner. He seems to have considered agriculture a pursuit quite beneath his dignity: the real sphere of his activities, he regarded as confined, for the most part, to war, hunting, fishing, and trade.

On the other hand, the great importance of the Iroquois woman as a producer lay in her activity as an agriculturist.[3] Although the men may have cleared the fields, the women sowed, cultivated, and harvested the crop. Even among the Hurons it was the women upon whom the responsibility fell. " Without wives," says a Huron to Le Jeune, " we are reduced to a wretched life, seeing that it is the women in our country who sow, plant, and cultivate the land, and prepare food for their husbands."[4] The Five Nations depended to an even greater extent upon their women to do the field work. " The women," says La Potherie, " sow, harvest and dry the Indian corn . . . . A man does not wish to marry any but a good worker."[5] Besides their agricultural labors, they attended to the gathering of the nuts, fruits and roots, which formed so important a part of the Iroquois food supply;[6] and they contributed, also, to the stock of implements to be used in production, by making traps for catching small ani-

[1] Lafitau, II, 78.

[2] Carr, " Mounds," Sm. Inst. Rep., 1891, pp. 516 sq.

[3] Lawson, " Carolina," p. 188; Schoolcraft, " Hist. Ind. Tribes," III, 191; Jes. Rel., XXXVIII, 255.

[4] Jes. Rel., XIV, 235.

[5] La Potherie, III, 19–20; Colden, " Hist. Five Nations " (London, 1747), p. 13—" The Indian women plant the corn and labor it in every respect till it is brought to the table."

[6] La Potherie, III, 19–20—" Elles vont chercher les fruits dans les campagnes . . . elles font des Trapes pour prendre les martes."

mals.[2] Furthermore, they manufactured many of the household utensils and furnishings. All the pottery was made by the women,[1] as were also the wooden mortars in which corn was crushed.[2] Textile industries were largely in their hands, from the gathering of the raw material to its final weaving into mats, baskets, etc.[3] In the making of clothing, also, the women took the chief part. Finally, to quote from the Jesuit Relation, "it is the woman who bears the burden of the house, cuts and carries the fire-wood, does the cooking, and loads herself on the journeys with provisions, etc., for the husband."[4] Bearing the burden of the house, and doing the cooking, was indeed no light task. It involved the making of trips into the winter woods, sometimes for a distance of many miles, to bring back the venison that the men had killed;[5] it meant the laborious smoking and drying of the meat and fish,[6] and the preparation of various things to be used in cooking. Evidently there was among the Iroquois a very distinct division of labor along sexual lines, the men acting chiefly as hunters and warriors, the women as agriculturists. Are we justified, however, in speaking of the men as if they did their work in coöperation with one another, and of the women as if they too formed a united production group?

Undoubtedly there were occasional instances in Iroquois life in which production seems to have been a purely individual and domestic affair. Snaring deer and other game in summer, when the animals are not gregarious and therefore cannot be hunted by large parties, was naturally done by each man for himself. Even in the regular hunting season, small family parties might wander off in the woods by themselves. Here and there we even find isolated women, each cultivating her own little plot of ground.

[1] Sagard, pp. 275-276; Schoolcraft, "Hist. Ind. Tribes," III, 81.

[2] La Potherie, III, 19-20.

[3] Jes. Rel., XIII, 265; XXIII, 55; Sagard, pp. 276-277.

[4] Jes. Rel., XXXVIII, 255; Schoolcraft, "Hist. Ind. Tribes," III, 191; Jes. Rel., LXIII, 219.

[5] Jes. Rel., LI, 129—"The women do hardly anything else all the winter but go and get the flesh of the deer or of the moose that the men have killed, sometimes fifty leagues away from the village."

[6] Jes. Rel., LVII, 267.

The Abbé de Galliné ran across one such case.[1] "On the eighth of August," he says, "we came to an island where a savage from the Seneca tribe has made a sort of country house whither he retires in summer to consume with his family some Indian corn and pumpkins that he raises there every year. He is so well hidden that unless one knew the place, one would have difficulty in finding it." This seems to be a real case of domestic economy.

In spite of such occasional exceptions the clan system seems to have been pretty well developed among the Iroquois and Hurons. "Indian habits and modes of life," says Mr. Morgan, "divided the people socially into two great classes, male and female. The male sought the conversation and society of the male, and they went forth together for amusement, or for the severer duties of life. In the same manner the female sought the companionship of her own sex."[2] Each group was in reality an organized body of individuals working in harmony.

As an organized body of workers, the women of each gens formed a distinct agricultural corporation. The fact has been pointed out that family groups, even in the domestic economy, are likely to remain together as long as their food-supply permits; also, that the aggregation of families is the very essence of the village economy. Among the Iroquois, however, the positive need of coöperation in production created out of each of these merely friendly aggregations a single united body, bound together by the strong ties of economic interest. Thus the women of an ordinary Iroquois village were organized in from three to eight clans, coincident with the feminine portions of the gentes. Similar conditions prevailed among the Hurons. "Each gens," says Major Powell, "has a right to the services of all its women in the cultivation of the soil."[3] Mary Jemison, the white woman brought up by the Iroquois, gives a detailed account of their methods. "In order to expedite their business," she says, "and at the same time enjoy each others' company, they all work to-

[1] Margry, I, 123. Cf. Jes. Rel., LII, 165.

[2] Morgan, "League," 323.

[3] Powell, Eth. Rep., 1879–1880, "Wyandot Gov't," p. 65.

gether in one field, or at whatever job they may have on hand. In the spring they choose an old active squaw to be their driver and overseer when at labor for the ensuing year. She accepts the honor, and they consider themselves bound to obey her. "When the time for planting arrives and the soil is prepared, the squaws are assembled in the morning, and conducted into a field, where each plants one row. They then go into the next field and plant one across, and so on till they have gone through the tribe (gens). If any remains to be planted, they again commence where they did at first in the same field, and so keep on till the whole is finished."[1] A similar account of the method of field-work practiced by the Iroquois women is given by Lafitau.[2] According to his statements, the weeding and cultivation of each plot during the summer was attended to by the individual possessors. The harvest operations, however, were carried on in the same way as the planting. "There is a time appointed for it (the harvest) when they all work together in common."

But the activities of the women's clan, as such, were not strictly limited to agricultural operations. In getting fire-wood the women employed coöperative methods. Among the Iroquois, according to Mary Jemison, "each squaw cuts her own wood, but it is all brought to the house under the direction of the overseer." "Among the Hurons," says Sagard, "all the women aid one another to make this provision of wood, which is done in the months of March and April, and with this order, in a little while each household is furnished with what is necessary."[3] In the same way, other occupations which permitted of it were carried on by the women's clans, rather than by individuals working separately. "By this rule," concludes Mary Jemison's account, "they perform their labor of every kind, and every jealousy of one having done more or less than another is effectually avoided."

Turning now to the men's part in production, we find that they, too, tended to work according to the coöperative plan. It is true

[1] Life of Mary Jemison, pp. 70–71.

[2] Lafitau, II, 75 sq. Cf. Jes. Rel., XXVI, 225.

[3] Sagard, 249; cf. Beauchamp, N. Y. St. Mus. Bul., No. 18, p. 12.

that forest hunting, pure and simple, usually results in the domestic, or at most, the village economy, rather than in the clan. Since the chief sources of food-supply roam the woods singly, or in small groups, society must be modelled after the same pattern; hence the Algonquins of the Northern Forest often hunted alone or in small bands of three or four hunters with their families. The clan organization appeared only occasionally, as the result of the necessity of defense. The Iroquois men were also forest hunters: nevertheless, there were reasons why they tended to organize in clans. In the first place, the peaceful agricultural settlements localized by the women, needed constant protection from marauders; this was the primary reason for the existence of the men's clan, an organization further strengthened by never-ending offensive campaigns: in the second place, game was plentiful in the Iroquois country, and the region itself was a park-like one; hence coöperative hunting by large parties of men paid better than could have been the case among the Algonquins in the denser and colder forest of the North. As a consequence, the military clan was a necessity. The hunting clan, on the other hand, was a possibility, rendered practicable by the nature of the environment and by the fact that the Iroquois men were already organized for purposes of warfare.

Primarily, the men's clan was coincident with the male portion of the gens. The Iroquois gens was a body of kindred organized into two clans mutually dependent upon each other for certain services. Similarly, among the Hurons, " each gens," according to Major Powell, " had the right to the service of all the male members in avenging wrongs,"[1] just as it had the right to the service of its female members in the cultivation of the fields. As a general thing, however, all the warriors' clans in each village acted as one body as far as such coöperation was advantageous. The Jesuit Relation mentions one case where a band of women were assailed as they were going out to their fields. At their first cries, all the warriors in the village rushed to their rescue.[2] At

[1] Eth. Rep., 1879-1880, " Wyandot Gov't," p. 65. Cf. Morgan, " Anc. Soc.," p. 71; Jes. Rel., XXXIX, 203.

[2] Jes. Rel., XXIX, 249.

another time, when a Huron village was attacked, the women fled, while the men—about one hundred warriors—united their forces and stayed behind to fight. In a word, to be a good warrior, and to aid in the preservation of his gens and his village was the chief object in the life of the Iroquois male.[1] To this end he was trained from his early childhood; " . . . infantile bands, armed with hatchets and guns which they can hardly carry . . . spread fear and horror everywhere," says the Jesuit Relation.[2] All able-bodied males between twenty and fifty years were regarded as warriors.[3] To shirk the duty meant disgrace, while to be a good warrior was of all things most honorable. To keep up the organization long expeditions were undertaken, lasting sometimes for months and even years.[4] At any time the warriors might be called upon to fall into line and fight, either as a whole or merely in volunteer bands of all sizes, bound upon errands of aggression or vengeance. Coöperation within these bands was of the closest sort.[5] Each warrior or group of warriors had some special duty to fulfill under the direction of the leader. In an expedition, some would hunt and supply meat for the troop, others would act as scouts, while still others would paddle the canoes and care for the rolls of bark out of which temporary shelters were made. All would meet at night in an appointed place. There, some would set up the tents, and others would cook the food. On approaching the enemy's country, the whole troop marched single file, covering their track with leaves. Though most Indian fighting was carried on in the woods, each warrior sheltering himself as best he could behind a tree or rock, nevertheless the Iroquois

[1] Jes. Rel., X, 225; XLI, 107; "Life of Mary Jemison," p. 187; Schoolcraft, "Notes on the Iroquois," pp. 150 sq.; Lafitau, II, 162 sq.

[2] Jes. Rel., XLIII, 263–265.

[3] La Hontan, "Voyages," II, 175—"A l'age de 20 ans, ils commencent à endosser le harnois, et le quittent à leur cinquantième année. S'ils portent les armes plutôt on plus tard ce n'est que pour marauder, mais ils ne sont point compris dans le nombre des guerriers."

Cf. Schoolcraft, "Notes on Iroquois," p. 83.

[4] Chadwick, "People of the Longhouse," p. 61; Jes. Rel., XIV, 39—"A sufficient garrison was left in the village."

[5] Schoolcraft, "Hist. Ind. Tribes," IV, 200; Lafitau, II, 162 sq.

often planned and followed out regular concerted evolutions in which each warrior had his fixed place. In bringing or sustaining a siege, the Iroquois soldiers worked together with the same foresight and careful planning.[1] We may imagine that the following quotation describes the siege of a Huron town by the Iroquois. "The siege of places where they find resistance," says Lafitau, "is again a proof that they have rules of an art of war, where skill and industry go hand in hand with force and the most intrepid bravery. If the besiegers make the most incredible efforts to surprise the vigilance of the besieged and to conquer all the obstacles that oppose them, the latter omit nothing which could serve them in making a good defense; feints, false attacks, vigorous and unforeseen sorties, ambushes, surprises,—everything is employed by both sides in war. But there are few sieges of long duration. The palisades being only of wood, and the cabins of bark, in vain do the besieged stock their ramparts with stones, beams and water, in vain do they repulse their assailants with a hail of arrows; the latter bring ruin to them with flaming arrows, a small number of which suffices, if the wind is favorable, to reduce the whole village to ashes. They make their approach fearlessly with coverings made of boards which they carry before them, and thanks to which they advance to the foot of the palisade which they break down with their axes or with fire. Or, they may make a counter-palisade, which serves them as a shield and as ladders, giving them the means of scaling the enemies' entrenchment and making themselves masters of it."

The clan spirit, brought about by this kind of coöperative activity, entirely overshadowed all othern motives. Family affection was as nothing before it. Thus Loskiel tells us:[2] "When the children and other kindred go to meet the father of a family after a long absence, he passes them with a haughty air, never returns their salutation, nor asks how his children do; for circumstances relating to his own family and kinsmen seem indifferent to him in time of war." Mr. Morgan[3] furnishes similar evidence. He says that the tie between father and children was

[1] Jes. Rel., XL, 103; Lafitau, II, 252–253.

[2] Loskiel, p. 59.

[3] Morgan, "League," p. 325.

very slight; "but when his sons grew up to maturity he became more attached to them, making them his companions in the hunt and upon the war-path."

It seems only natural that men in whose minds warfare had already cultivated the clan idea were inclined as far as possible to employ the same principle in everything they did; hence, even in the village, the men's clans as such carried on a certain amount of direct production. According to Lafitau, when a lodge is to be erected, "the youth of the village are invited, a feast is given to encourage them, and in less than a couple of days the whole work is done."[1] Then, too, the men must have coöperated in clearing the land for the village; they certainly did so in the work of fortifying the town.[2]

We are not surprised, therefore, upon considering their military habits, and the favorable nature of their environment, to hear that the Iroquois tended to employ the clan method even in their hunting.[3] An army on the march was, as we have seen, often at the same time a hunting party, and *vice versa*.[4] But organized companies were also in the habit of forming purely for hunting purposes. Mr. Morgan describes a favorite method of securing game: ". . . A large party of hunters was formed and a brush fence was built in the shape of the letter V, two or three miles in length on each side. The woods were then fired in the rear at some miles distant, so as to drive the deer toward the opening, into which they were guided by parties stationed upon either side. They followed the fence down to the angle, where the

[1] Lafitau, II, 11.

[2] Jes. Rel., X, 203.

[3] LaHontan, "Voyages," II, 93—"Les Iroquois sont plus grands, plus vaillants, et plus rusez que les autres peuples, mais moins agiles et moins adroits, tant à la guerre qu' à la chasse, où ils ne vont jamais qu'en grand nombre."

Cf. Perrot, p. 54; Loskiel, pp. 78–79; Jes. Rel., XII, 273.

[4] Jes. Rel., XXIV, 123; Jes. Rel., LIV, 73—"The ideas of all these tribes prompt them to the pursuit of nothing but hunting and warfare. Among them are seen only parties of twenty, thirty, or fifty men, of a hundred or sometimes two hundred; rarely do they go to the number of a thousand in a single band. These bands are divided, to go some in quest of men, and others in quest of beasts."

arrows of the unseen hunters soon brought them down one after the other. Sometimes a hundred were thus taken at one time." [1] These coöperating groups might be composed of men alone, as for instance, when the young men went out from the village for a day or two at a time; or they might be accompanied by women and children. The latter was usual during the long winter hunt. [2] In the latter case the women did not go as a clan, but merely as dependents of individual members of the men's organization. Thus, while in the productive life of the village the men's clan as the garrison played a part somewhat subordinate to that taken by the women's clan, during the hunting expedition the situation was reversed. Here control of the access to the source of supply, as well as the defense of the group, was in the hands of the men's clan, and consequently the women's organization entirely disintegrated.

The same thing occurred in the fishing season. Wherever coöperation was advantageous, the men worked according to that method, while the women acted in a subordinate capacity.[3] More or less fishing was always carried on in conjunction with hunting,[4] but there were also many large and lengthy expeditions which had fishing as their sole purpose.[5] Sometimes as many as three hundred to four hundred would go together and pitch their temporary camps on the same spot. Between the male members of such parties considerable coöperation would spring up. Among the Hurons seine-fishing was carried on by large parties, working harmoniously together.[6] Everywhere the building and use of weirs and hurdles involved considerable coöperation.[7] Loskiel mentions a case of the sort. A large net, made of a rope of wild

[1] Morgan, "League," p. 345.

[2] Jes. Rel., LIV, 117; LVII, 261; LVIII, 83; LV, 253, 255, 269; XXXI, 71; XXXIII, 83; XXXIV, 87.

[3] Jes. Rel., LVII, 267.

[4] Loskiel, p. 94—"The Indians always carry hooks and small harpoons with them, whenever they are on a hunting party."

[5] Jes. Rel., XXXIX, 215; XV, 113, 125; XIX, 87; LIII, 243; XXVI, 41; LII, 175; LIV, 81.

[6] Jes. Rel., XVII, 197.

[7] Beauchamp, N. Y. St. Mus. Bul., No. 16, p. 197.

vine with a fringe of branches about six feet long, was used to sweep a stream; some members of the party walking along each bank held the ends of the wild-vine rope, and others supported the middle with wooden forks; at the weir, men standing on each side of the central opening, with poles and shouts drove the fish into a large perforated box; then other Indians stationed in canoes on each side took out the fish. Sometimes by this method more than one thousand were caught in half a day.[1]

The Iroquois method of production, then, was a double one. In the village, control of the surplus was shared between the men's and the women's clans—the latter carrying on most of the work of production; the former acting singly or collectively as a military guard. In the war and hunting expeditions, the women's clan entirely disappeared; yet in the general life of the community, the latter occupied the more important place. The reasons were two: in the first place, agriculture, the branch of production controlled by the women's clan, was becoming the chief dependence of the whole nation—more and more as the years went on, the Iroquois took on the characteristics of sedentary villagers living mainly on the produce of their cornfields; in the second place, the very nature of the work of the two clans gave the women's organization a decided advantage; fishing and hunting often did not allow extensive coöperation; hence, even in the hunting season, the men's clan economy might at any time give way before conditions demanding the adoption of the village or domestic system. Warfare, of course, absolutely demanded coöperation; nevertheless, it permitted great variations in the size and personnel of the band. In theory, the men of each gens formed a clan whose chief duty was the protection of its sister clan and of itself; in practice the clan was composed of rather unstable elements, the different objects to be accomplished determining in each case the number and make-up of the group. Often a small expedition might be made up of members of several different gentes. The women's clan, on the other hand, always presented an unchanged front. It had a definite task to perform, the magnitude of which did not vary much from year to year,

[1] Loskiel, p. 95; cf. Beauchamp, "Iroquois Trail," p. 92.

and in which coöperation was always advantageous; every summer, the same amount of work, done upon the same spot, resulted in about the same product as in the year before: hence the female clan need never vary in membership or size; neither must it wander from place to place. It would be no wonder, therefore, if in regard to its influence upon the general character of the community, the men's clan should tend to occupy a position subordinate to that held by their sister organization.

Economic conditions led to the organization of the Iroquois into clans: for similar reasons these smaller bodies were at the same time united in one large body, namely, the Tribe. The main motive for tribal organization was the necessity of defense. For this purpose, the tribe possessed the right to the services of all its male members. The actual strength of the army varied with circumstances. In times of peace the tribe tended to disintegrate and make scattered settlements, generally with some one gens predominating in each. In seasons of disturbance and alarm, there was likely to be only one great village in which the separate life of the gentes was merged in that of the whole. Once brought together by the necessity of close coöperation in defense, the tribal organization was strengthened by various other factors. The propitiation of forces controlling the weather was a strong bond of union, often in itself an effectual motive for combination. When any one was drowned or frozen to death, the Hurons believed that the sky was angry and instituted a series of sacrifices and feasts. According to the Jesuit Relation, "A gathering of the neighboring villages takes place, many feasts are made, and no presents are spared, as it is a matter in which the whole country is interested."[1] A similar effect was caused by the necessity of common action to ward off epidemics. In such cases representatives of the warriors would feast together, and their example would be followed by the representatives of the women, some from each clan.[2] Again, there was the constant danger of

[1] Jes. Rel., X, 163.

[2] Jes. Rel., XIII, 237; cf. Jes. Rel., X, 219—"Here you cannot insult any one of them without the whole country resenting it, and taking up the quarrel against you, and even against an entire village."

a fire in which the whole village might be destroyed. Every inhabitant, at such a crisis, was *de facto* a member of the fire-brigade. All these motives combined to cause a federation of the clans, and an organization of economic life from the point of view of the tribe.

The formation of the Iroquois into clans and tribes was the result of their primitive struggle for economic prosperity. Their organization into a confederacy of tribes, though an affair of much later date, had similar reasons for being. An understanding of some sort was indeed to be expected between tribes living next door to each other in a region marked off as a distinct geographic unity, speaking the same language, and standing on the same level of culture. In fact, the Iroquois soon became aware that the common enjoyment of utilities meant greater economic benefit for all, and that in union, rather than in individual independence, lay the secret of power against outside nations. The Hurons, to the north of them, were not long in recognizing the same fact. Among the latter the movement never went further than the formation of a mere league.[1] The Iroquois, however, created a well organized Confederacy. Mr. Morgan was so impressed by the completeness of the Iroquois' plan of federation that he believed it to embody the well thought-out scheme of some one great leader. The truth seems to be that the Confederacy was the growth of many years.[2] As early, perhaps, as

Jes. Rel., X, 211 sq.—"They maintain themselves in this perfect harmony by frequent visits, by help they give one another in sickness, by feasts and by alliances."

[1] Jes. Rel. XVII, 195; XVI, 227.

Other examples of such confederacies as the Iroquois and Hurons may be seen in that of the Creeks, consisting of six tribes; the Ottawa Confederacy (3 tribes); the Dakota League of the "Seven Council Fires." Morgan, "Anc. Soc.," p. 122.

[2] Parkman, "Christian Examiner," May, 1851—"The divided Iroquois harassed by the attacks of enemies, or threatened by a general inroad, might have been led to see the advantages of a league; and to effect that end, the most simple and obvious course would have been that the sachems of all the nations should unite in a common council. When this had been done, when a few functionaries had been appointed, and certain necessary regulations established, the league would have formed itself, without any

the year 1450, the Onondagas, Oneidas, Cayugas, and Senecas were united in an offensive and defensive league; a hundred years later, the Mohawks arrived and settled permanently in the Mohawk Valley; and by 1570 the league had probably taken its historic form.

Besides the Iroquois themselves, with their clan, their tribal and their confederate organization, there was also another class of producers to be found in every Iroquois village. This element in the population was composed of captives—slaves, the Jesuits call them—and of some other persons of servile status. Slave labor, in a modified form, was employed by members of both men's and women's clans. Captives, whose lives had been spared for this purpose, did the hardest and most menial work in every line of production—in hunting and fishing, in agriculture, and in housework. "It was an Iroquois custom," says Mr. Carr, "to use captives to assist their women in the labors of the field, in carrying burdens, and in doing general menial labor."[1] Thus we hear of a certain mistress of twenty slaves who "knew not what it was to go to the forest to get wood, nor to the river to draw water."[2] Deserving captives were eventually admitted to clan membership.[3] Nevertheless, at any given moment there were always two elements in the Iroquois population: on the one hand, the free producers, organized into clans and controlling the access to the sources of supply; on the other hand, the captives—an aggregation of individuals completely in the power of their conquerors. The other element in the servile class was composed

very elaborate legislation, in the condition in which it stood at the time of its highest prosperity. To these views Morgan assents in his last word upon the subject."

[1] Carr, "Mounds," Sm. Inst. Rep., 1891, p. 517. Cf. La Hontan, "Voyages," II, 7—"Women slaves are employed to sow and reap the Indian corn; the men slaves have for their business the hunting and shooting when there is any fatigue." Cf. Jes. Rel., XVI, 201; XXXI, 61, 71, 81; XXXIV, 117; XXXIX, 63, 187; LX, 185; II, 298.

[2] Jes Rel., LIV, 93.

[3] Carr, "Mounds," Sm. Inst. Rep., 1891, p. 517—"When a captive proved himself possessed of what in their judgment constituted manly qualities, then he was fully adopted and admitted to all the privileges of an Iroquois."

of certain effeminate men of Iroquois birth. These persons, often perfectly able-bodied, but too self-indulgent to endure the hardships of hunting and war, had abandoned the men's clan and devoted themselves to field-work and other feminine occupations. Their desertion of the sphere of activity in which they were most needed was punished by contempt and scorn. According to Ely S. Parker, an educated Iroquois, "when any man, excepting the cripples, old men, and those disabled in war or hunting, chose to till the earth, he was at once ostracised from men's society, classed as a woman or squaw, and disqualified from sitting or speaking in the councils of his people until he had redeemed himself by becoming a skillful warrior or a successful hunter."[1] Effeminate men and captives thus formed a servile class producing under the direction and authority of the clans.

At the same time there was arising, within the clan, a class of persons who, by virtue of the part they claimed to play in production, had a certain indefinite authority over the activities of the clan itself. The medicine men were the supposed masters of certain natural forces, without whose aid all labor would be in vain. No crop could succeed nor hunting expedition prosper, unless the medicine man exerted himself to bring good weather. At every turn the coöperation of the medicine man was necessary for the welfare of the clan. Just as the clans directed the labor and controlled every action of the servile classes, so the medicine men, in their turn, determined to a certain extent the ultimate fate of the clans.

To recapitulate:—the nature of their environment caused the Iroquois to pursue hunting and fishing, and even to a greater extent, agriculture, as a means of livelihood: a sexual division of labor resulted, the women devoting themselves mainly to agriculture, the men to warfare and hunting: within these groups,

[1] Carr, "Mounds," Sm. Inst. Rep., 1891, p. 517. The class of males in question existed in many semi-agricultural and hunting tribes in America. They rose in public estimation as the community tended more and more to go over to the agricultural basis and the work of the hunter and warrior became less important. Among the Illinois, for instance, the effeminate men were summoned to the councils and held in great respect. Jes. Rel., LIX, 129, p. 309, note 26.

coöperative methods of work were found advantageous, and hence the formation of the women's and of the men's clans—the former to carry on agriculture; the latter to attend to war and hunting: for reasons arising from the very nature of their work, and the differing degrees of importance of their product, the women's clan had a more conspicuous influence on the life of the community than the men's organization: altogether, the transitional stage of culture upon which the Iroquois were living, affords a valuable opportunity for the simultaneous study of the economy regulated by the hunting and warring clan of men, and of the first stages of the economy dominated by the communal clan: economic conditions, also, account for the organization of the clans into tribes, and of the latter into a confederacy: finally, the fact is patent that besides the Iroquois proper with their clan, tribal, and confederate organization, there also existed another class of producers, composed of captives and effeminate men, whose relation to the Iroquois was a coercive one, based upon the fact that their personal liberty was controlled by the clans: in addition, there were the medicine men who also exercised a sort of coercion over the clans; their power, based upon their supposed monopoly of the control of certain natural forces, being coextensive with the degree of credulity of the people.

CHAPTER IV.

THE WEALTH OF THE IROQUOIS.

The wealth of the Iroquois, gained largely by coöperative effort, and without any private appropriation of the sources of supply, consisted of a heterogeneous collection of economic goods. Since there was no recognized standard in units of which the sum of values could be expressed, the Iroquois always considered their wealth in the concrete, as a relatively valuable collection of goods. Some of these were useful as production, others as direct consumption goods.

Among the production-goods of the Iroquois, there were certain implements of general use in forest life, while others owed their existence to the prevalence of some particular manner of producing raw material. All these articles, however, may be termed primary production-goods.

The simplest, and at the same time the most universally necessary implement in use among the Iroquois, as among all primitive peoples, was the knife.[1] In nearly all productive operations it was the first tool needed; fortunately, it was also the most easily obtained. "If a knife was wanted," says Mr. Beauchamp, "a flake was picked up, to which in a few minutes an edge was given; it was used and thrown away.[2] Larger and more carefully worked specimens of stone, bone, or wood were also made and preserved for permanent use. Among those of stone, some were nearly circular, and chipped to a sharp edge all around; others were elliptical, or of long diamond form; many approached what we call the knife form, being long and narrow, thin and sharp, and inserted in a handle. Such an implement would be

[1] Beauchamp, N. Y. St. Mus. Bul., No. 16, p. 49–53; No. 41, pp. 378–379; No. 50, p. 255; Morgan, "League," p. 358.

[2] Beauchamp, N. Y. St. Mus. Bul., No. 16, p. 15.

useful alike in war, in hunting, and in many other activities of daily life.

Side by side with the knife in the scale of importance, stands the axe. This also was a tool whose services were needed at one stage or another of almost every branch of production. The axe, or celt, one of the few polished stone articles made by the Iroquois, was a piece of hard sandstone, greenstone, or slate,[1] chipped and polished into the shape of an ordinary hatchet or wedge, round and blunt at one end, and with a broad cutting edge at the other. "Often" says Lafitau,[2] "the life time of a savage was not long enough for its completion; whence it comes that such an article, though still rude and imperfect, was a precious heritage for the children." The putting on of the handle was, in itself, no small task. "One must choose a young tree," Lafitau goes on to tell us, "and without cutting it down, make a handle of it. One cuts it in one end and there inserts the stone; the tree grows, presses it tight, and so incorporates it in its trunk that it is rare and difficult to remove it." At this stage of growth the tree was cut down and the axe and its wooden handle were carved out, ready for use. Sometimes, however, the handle seems to have been put on by quicker and more artificial methods; the orifice of the only ancient handle now in possession of the New York State Museum has evidently been finished, at least, by fire.[3] Mr. Morgan says that a deep groove was cut around the small end of the hatchet, by means of which it was firmly attached to the handle with a withe or thong.[4] This statement, however, does not seem to be well founded, either upon historical or archeological evidence. Instead of the groove, the device of roughening the stone near the blunt end was adopted by the Iroquois, in order to give the handle a firm grip. These axes were used to fell trees, to cut fire-wood, and for other work of the sort. Fire was generally employed to do the first part of the work, the stone tool being used to chip away the charred wood. We learn from

[1] Beauchamp, N. Y. St. Mus. Bul., No. 18, pp. 11 sq.
[2] Lafitau, II, 110.
[3] Beauchamp, N. Y. St. Mus. Bul., No. 18, p. 12.
[4] Morgan, "League," p. 359.

Champlain, however, that the axe sometimes did the whole work, and did it much more expeditiously than would seem likely to a modern lumberman. Champlain says that the Mohawks in 1609, upon meeting his party, "began to hew down trees with villanous axes which they sometimes got in war, and others of stone, and fortified themselves very securely."

Besides such implements of general usefulness as the axe and the knife, the Iroquois manufactured others especially intended to increase the products of hunting, fishing, and agriculture. The implement most important to the hunter was his bow and arrow. The bow was made of red cedar or some similar wood, hardened by fire and scraped into shape with a shell knife.[1] It was not the short bow, so efficient in the hands of the mounted hunter; on the contrary, it often equalled the height of a man.[2] A weapon of this kind could be used only by a man of strength and experience. In such hands it could send an arrow with fearful force. The bow string consisted of a hempen cord or a deer sinew. If the latter, it was prepared by being drawn back and forth in a groove cut in a piece of soft sandstone.[3] The arrow used was about three feet long. Sometimes two feathers stripped from the quill were passed around the small end in a twist and tied in place with sinews. This arrangement caused the arrow to revolve in its flight, giving it a horizontality and precision of motion which much increased its force. In this respect, the Iroquois hunter showed greater ingenuity than was displayed by the English and Scottish archers who never seemed to have discovered the advantages to be secured by a revolving motion of the arrow.[4] It is probable, however, that the Iroquois did not always make use of their invention, since a rotary motion often may not have been desirable in the woods. The Iroquois arrow-head was made of wood, stone, or bone: the

[1] Beauchamp, N. Y. St. Mus. Bul., No. 16, p. 41.

[2] Beauchamp, N. Y. St. Mus. Bul., No. 16, p. 46; Lafitau, II, 196; Morgan, "League," pp. 305-306.

[3] Beauchamp, N. Y. St. Mus. Bul., No. 18, p. 43.

[4] Beauchamp, N. Y. St. Mus. Bul., No. 16, pp. 24-25; Morgan, "League," pp. 305-306.

Onondagas, according to Mr. Beauchamp, now use, and probably always have used, blunt headed arrows made entirely of wood: stone arrow-heads, however, seem to have been most commonly employed by the other tribes. These last were generally of the common flint of the region, chipped into a flat triangular shape. Less frequent than the stone were the bone and horn arrow-heads. These were sometimes merely hollow points into which the wooden shaft was fitted, and less often were solid pieces inserted into the wood. Most of the Iroquois arrow-heads, of whatever material, were barbed and fastened to the shaft with a strong fish glue, or bound on with sinew and cord.[1]

Traps and snares were much used by the Iroquois hunter.[2] They were generally made with the aid of strong bark or hempen ropes and cords.[3] Mr. Morgan describes one species of deer trap, in which a young tree was bent over, and so adjusted that the springing of the trap fastened a loop around the hind legs of the animal, and at the same time released the tree, thus drawing the deer upwards and holding him suspended in the air.[4] La Hontan says that foxes, bears, martens and some other varieties of game were also generally caught in traps.[5] Beaver were rarely taken by this method, as the only kind of trap that could deceive them was made of a sort of willow very hard to get. Their own dam, in fact, when a hole had been cut in it and the water allowed to run out, formed an effective enough trap in which they could be killed with ease. In winter, however, they were often caught in nets spread under holes in the ice and baited with a bit of wood. Another use of the net was as a snare for wild fowl. According to La Potherie, the Iroquois used to "make a broad path in the woods, and attach to two trees, one on each side, a large net in the shape of a sack well opened."[6] Sometimes seven or eight

[1] Beauchamp, N. Y. St. Mus. Bul., No. 16, pp. 15-38; No. 50, pp. 290-293; Lafitau, II, 196.

[2] Jes. Rel., XXIX, 207; XXIII, 157.

[3] Jes. Rel., IX, 253.

[4] Morgan, "League," p. 345.

[5] La Hontan, "Voyages," II, 160.

[6] La Potherie, II, 80.

hundred pigeons were thus captured in[1] one night. Mr. Morgan describes a contrivance for corraling deer, which is based upon somewhat the same principle as the net for capturing birds. He also says that the Iroquois had no dogs adapted to the chase; yet when we consider the universal use of dogs for hunting purposes by all the other forest tribes, we cannot believe that they alone bred dogs only as articles of food. We are certain, at any rate, that the Hurons trained dogs to aid in the pursuit and capture of game, and that they valued them for this purpose even more than as food.[2]

The bow and arrow, traps and snares of various kinds, and perhaps the dog, were then the chief means of production used by the Iroquois hunter.

Fishing also necessitated the creation of a distinct set of implements, the most characteristic of which were the harpoon and the net. Although large fish were frequently shot with an arrow by a man wading in a shallow stream or standing in the bow of a canoe,[3] yet the harpoon[4] was the weapon most often in the hands of the fisherman. It was made of bone or horn, pointed and barbed on one side or on both. The size varied: one fine specimen lately found on a village site in Monroe County, N. Y.—a single-barbed harpoon of elk-horn—measured nearly 10½ inches in length, and was about half an inch broad in the middle. Such a head, attached to a stout staff, might do great execution in the hands of a skillful fisherman. La Jeune says that "in the eel season a man might spear three hundred in a single night." Fish-hooks do not seem to have been used to any great extent before the coming of the whites;[6] nevertheless, a sort of bone hook was made, differing somewhat from that manufactured afterwards from the European model. Sagard describes the primitive

[1] Jes. Rel., XLII, 95; LVI, 49.

[2] Jes. Rel., VI, 299, 303; XIV, 33; LVII, 299, 319; LXIII, 265; LX, 153.

[3] Beauchamp, N. Y. St. Mus. Bul., No. 16, p. 19.

[4] *Ibid.*, No. 50, p. 293-304.

[5] Jes. Rel., VI, 309.

[6] Beauchamp, N. Y. St. Mus. Bul., No. 50, pp. 304-311; Beauchamp, "Iroquois Trail," pp. 92-93.

Huron invention as "a piece of wood and a bone, so placed as to form a hook, and very neatly bound together with hemp." Just how these articles were made we get no very good idea; at any rate, it seems certain that they were not much used. Besides the harpoon, the net was the chief implement used in fishing. The article itself was the product of considerable labor, involving the gathering and preparation of the hemp or bark fiber and its weaving into the desired fabric. The aid given by the net to the fisherman, however, repaid him for the time and pains spent in its manufacture. All the Iroquois made extensive use of the net, especially in the capture of smaller fish in the rifts and shallow places of streams where most of their fishing camps were situated. Here they could employ their favorite implement, either as a scoop-net or as a seine. Nets were used both summer and winter. The Hurons used to fish by this means through holes cut in the ice.[1] The utility of both nets and harpoons was greatly increased by the use of weirs of various kinds within which the fish were driven in great numbers.[2] The Hurons often placed hurdles in streams, with nets across the openings. The Oneidas, according to Mr. Beauchamp, "made fish-pounds with two rows of stakes across streams, driving the fish into them and killing them there." The Iroquois also built stone fish-weirs, one of which is still standing in the Seneca River—a stone wall several hundred feet in extent, and built zig-zag across the river. Considerable ingenuity was displayed in the construction of these weirs. In 1656–7 the Jesuit Chronicler admiringly remarks: "Our savages construct their dams and sluices so well that they catch at the same time the eels that descend and the salmon that always ascend."[3]

Just as hunting and fishing led to the invention of certain implements of use in these pursuits, so also the practice of agriculture caused the employment of another special set of tools. After

[1] Sagard, p. 259; Jes. Rel., XXXV, 175.
Beauchamp, N. Y. St. Mus. Bul., No. 16, p. 75; Beauchamp, "Iroquois Trail," pp. 92–93; La Potherie, III, 34.

[2] Beauchamp, N. Y. St. Mus. Bul., No. 16, pp. 76–78.

[3] Jes. Rel., XLIII, 261.

the fire and the axe[1] had been made to do their part in clearing the land, rakes, in the shape of a big wooden hook, were employed to drag the brush-wood along the ground to the heap where it was to be burned. In the roughly prepared ground, between the roots and stumps of the trees, corn hills about three feet in diameter and standing well apart were heaped up by the aid of another wooden tool. Lafitau describes this tool as "a curved piece of wood, three fingers broad, attached to a long handle."[2] With this digging stick eight or nine holes were made in a hill, and filled up again after the seed had been dropped in. Cultivation was carried on mostly with wooden hoes:[3] sometimes a shell or the shoulder blade of a deer, fastened to a wooden handle, might be used instead.

Thus each of the great productive activities of the Iroquois led to the invention of certain necessary implements. Because they were hunters, they used the bow and arrow and traps of various kinds; because they were fishers they developed the idea of the harpoon, the net and the weir; as agriculturists they invented the rake, the digging stick, and the hoe; and in every branch of production, they used the knife and the axe. All these implements were of the most simple and primitive construction; nevertheless, they were made of the most available and easily manufactured material, and were exactly what was needed for the particular purpose for which they were invented.

Since the articles thus far mentioned were the means of producing raw materials, they have been called primary production-goods. The subsequent working up of these raw products into finished consumption-goods demanded the invention of another set of implements, which may be designated secondary production-goods.

First on the list were the articles used in the preparation of food. To kindle the fire over which they cooked or smoked their provisions, the Iroquois used the weighted drill with spindle-

[1] La Potherie, III, 18–19; Lafitau, II, 109–110; Champlain, p. 86.
[2] Lafitau, II, 75 sq.; La Potherie, III, 19.
[3] Beauchamp, N. Y. St. Mus. Bul., No. 16, p. 54; No. 18, p. 24.

whorl.[1] Cooking and eating utensils, though simple, were made of the best available material—chiefly bark, wood and earthenware—and fulfilled very satisfactorily the purposes for which they were intended. "Our cooking and eating utensils," says Mary Jemison, "consisted of a hominy block and pestle, a small kettle, a knife or two, and a few vessels of bark or wood."[2] The mortar and pestle were among the most important articles of household furniture. The former, though sometimes made of stone, was usually a tree trunk hollowed out by fire, while the pestle was a piece of hard wood, larger at both ends and smaller in the middle. The wooden mortar was used to grind corn and dried meats, while the stone mortar served to crush nut shells, materials for pottery, and other hard substances.[3] Next to the mortar in importance came the earthenware vessels in which the cooking was done. These pots, made of clay mixed with pounded stone and shell, were spherical at the bottom, and usually constricted below the top, having an expanded rim. There were two sorts,—common clay colored pottery, and the more valuable black pottery, which was of fine enough texture to admit of a polish, and firm enough to look like stone. According to Sagard, the material, with a little grease added to it, was worked and kneaded by the hands of the women into a perfectly rounded ball. With the fist, a hole was then made in the material and constantly enlarged by turning and slapping the outside of the mass with a little wooden paddle, until the vessel had assumed the desired shape. It was then dried in the sun and baked in a fire made of bark. "These vessels," Sagard says, "are so strong that they do not break when on the fire without water in them, as ours do, but at the same time they cannot stand dampness and cold water long without getting frail and breaking at the least knock that one gives them. Otherwise they are very durable."[4] The early writers mention only the method of making pottery described by

[1] Mason, "Origin of Inventions," p. 88.
[2] "Life of Mary Jemison," p. 72.
[3] La Potherie, III, 19; Beauchamp, N. Y. St. Mus. Bul., No. 18, p. 32, 34.
[4] Sagard, pp. 275-276.

Sagard. Mr. Beauchamp thinks that vessels were sometimes formed on a kind of foundation, though just what it might have been, he does not know. In general the hand seems to have been employed without much other aid. The method of cooking, whether by placing the vessel on the fire, or by putting red hot stones in it until the contents were brought to the boiling point, is also a matter of doubt. From Sagard's account, the former method seems probable. These pots were also used for other purposes than the primary one of cooking. They were probably employed as water-pails or for holding a temporary supply of grain. For the reception of dry substances, however, the bark dish, tray, or barrel was most convenient. The bark tray was used in a number of ways, but chiefly in the preparation of corn-bread. It was made of a strip of elm-bark, rounded or gathered up at the ends, so as to form a shallow concavity. Around the rim, splints of hickory were stitched to hold the article in shape. These trays were of all sizes, holding from one to ten pecks.[1] The bark tub for holding maple sap and for other similar uses was made in somewhat the same way.[2] The bark barrel in which surplus stores were kept was also made of the inner rind of the red-elm bark, the grain running around the barrel. It was stitched firmly up the side, and had the bottom and lid secured in the same manner.[3] It was very durable, and would last for years, if properly cared for. Other articles of wood or similar substances were the sieves used for sifting meal. These were made of twigs, splints, or corn-husks.[4] Splint baskets of all sizes were also manufactured. The articles used in eating were also mostly of wood or bark. Bowls, pitchers and other vessels of wood, plates of wood or of bark, spoons of wood and occasionally of bone or of horn were common in every Iroquois household.[5]

To sum up,—the apparatus for kindling the fire, the stone and

[1] Morgan, "League," p. 367.

[2] *Ibid.*, pp. 369–370.

[3] *Ibid.*, p. 366.

[4] *Ibid.*, pp. 382–383; Lafitau, II, 86–87.

[5] Beauchamp, N. Y. St. Mus. Bul., No. 50, pp. 315 sq.; Morgan, "League," p. 383; Lafitau, II, 87; Jes. Rel., XXXVIII, 247.

wooden mortars, a few earthenware vessels, bark and wooden trays, boxes, plates, and dishes, besides the ever necessary knife, were the chief instruments used by the Iroquois in the preparation of their food.

The making of clothing and coverings called for very little inventive genius on the part of the Iroquois. Their small textile industry they carried on almost entirely without the aid of tools. Lafitau and Morgan describe for us the process of manufacturing thread.[1] After the outer surface of the bark had been removed, the soft inner portion, cut into narrow strips with the finger-nail, was boiled in ashes and water. When dry, it was easily separated into small filaments several feet in length. These were then rolled with the palm of the hand on the bare knee into threads or cords of any thickness and length. Neither spinning wheels nor distaffs were used to work up the thread into textiles. Schoolcraft says that the reed mats and such fabrics were probably made with the help of a sort of bone shuttle, a specimen of which has been found near Fort Niagara, N. Y. This implement, intended to introduce the woof of the fabric, Schoolcraft describes as made "of finely polished bone. It is ten and a half inches in length, perfectly round, about one-eighth of an inch in thickness, and has a double-barbed head a quarter of an inch in length. Between the barbs is a mouth or slit which would enable it to carry the thread across and through the warp." [2] Another implement, employed in making burden straps and such articles, was a sort of hickory needle with which the bark thread was knit.[3] Aside from these simple tools, the Iroquois textile industry, limited as it was by the lack of any raw material like wool or cotton, did not necessitate the use of special implements. The manufacture of skin articles, though comparatively extensive, was also of a nature not likely to lead to many inventions. In the first place a wooden or stone scraper was necessary.[4] Gen-

[1] Lafitau, II, 159–160; Morgan, "League," pp. 364–366.
Cf. Sagard, pp. 250–251; Eth. Rep., 1891–'2, p. 23; La Potherie, III, 34.
[2] Schoolcraft, "Hist. Ind. Tribes," I, 88.
[3] Morgan, "League," p. 365.
[4] Morgan, "League," pp. 361–362.

erally, the Iroquois employed a wooden blade, avoiding here as elsewhere the unnecessary use of stone.[1] With this implement the hair and grain of the fresh deer skin was removed. This skin was then cured by soaking in a solution of deer brains and subsequent exposure to a smoky fire, until the pores were closed and the skin soft and pliable. Bone, horn, or wooden awls and needles, with thread of vegetable fibre or sinew, were then employed to sew the skin into the desired shape.[2] "A small bone near the ankle joint of the deer," says Mr. Morgan, "has furnished the moccason needle of time immemorial, and the sinews the thread."[3] Bone needles were generally flat and thin, often rounded at the ends, and having two holes near the centre. They were in fact, more like bodkins than real needles. Most of the finer work was probably done with the bone or horn awl, used as is a modern shoemaker's instrument.[4] A simple shuttle, and a wooden knitting needle, scrapers, and wooden and bone awls and bodkins, then, were the only inventions known or needed by the Iroquois for use in their textile industry and in the manufacture of skin articles.

Among secondary production-goods should also be mentioned a third class of inventions arising out of the necessity of transporting products of all sorts frequently from one spot to another. Fishing and hunting were generally carried on at a distance from the village, and the surplus product had to be carried home in order to be utilized; firewood and building materials often had to be brought from a spot a mile or so from the village; agricultural products were sometimes to be transported from fields some distance away from the village; and a general migration was occasionally necessary: hence came the invention of several articles to facilitate transportation by land and by water.

In the warm season, goods going by land routes had to be carried for the most part on the back of the individual himself. The task was facilitated, however, by the use of bretelles and

[1] Beauchamp, N. Y. St. Mus. Bul., No. 16, p. 64.
[2] Beauchamp, N. Y. St. Mus. Bul., No. 50, pp. 312–313. Lafitau, II, 160.
[3] Morgan, "League," pp. 360–361.
[4] Beauchamp, N. Y. St. Mus. Bul., No. 50, p. 311.

burden straps.[1] The former, according to Lafitau, were "a sort of wooden frame very convenient to lift a heavy load and carry it easily." If this were not at hand, the goods were made into a package and carried on the shoulders by means of a burden strap passed around the forehead or chest. The strap, woven with warp and woof of filaments of bark, was about fifteen feet long and three or four inches wide in the centre. In winter, when snow lay on the ground, the problem of land transportation was more easily solved. Under these circumstances the hunter himself travelled easily and swiftly with the aid of his snow-shoes, and at the same time dragged a heavily loaded sled. The snow-shoe, without which the hunter of the Eastern Forest would have been quite helpless in winter, and with which he could travel more easily than in summer, was a hickory framework three feet long and sixteen inches wide, bent round with an arching front and brought to a point at the heel. Cross pieces held it in shape. Within the area was a woven net-work of deer strings, with interstices about an inch square. To this the ball of the foot was lashed with thongs. The heel, however, was left free to work up and down, while through an opening left for them the toes could descend below the surface of the shoe as the heel was raised in the act of walking.[2] The sled, according to Lafitau,[3] "is made of two small and very slender boards, which both together are not more than a foot broad, and are six or seven feet long. The boards are bent upwards and turned backwards in front to a distance of about six inches, in order to break and turn aside the snow which, piling up, would prevent the sled from running easily. Two sticks, a little raised, run along the whole length of the sled on both sides, and are fastened to it at regular intervals. To them are attached the ropes which hold the load on the sled. A savage, with his collar passed over his chest, and wrapped in his blanket, draws his heavily laden sled after him without much difficulty."[4] Bretelles and burden-straps, snow-shoes and sleds, were

[1] Lafitau, II, 219; Morgan, "League," pp. 365–366.

[2] Morgan, "League," pp. 376–377.

[3] Lafitau, II, 216–217.

[4] Lafitau, II, 220.

the principal means invented by the Indian for transportation by land. For water travel they had the invaluable bark canoe. Birch bark suitable for the purpose did not grow in the Iroquois territory; hence the boats of their own manufacture were generally made of elm bark. A large piece of the latter material was shaped in canoe form, strengthened by a rim and ribs of white ash, stitched into place with thread or twine, and splints. Both ends of the canoe were alike sharp and vertical. The size varied from twelve to forty feet in length, with a seating capacity of from two to thirty people.[1] Mr. Morgan says that such a canoe would last several years if well cared for; but Lafitau, who knew the Iroquois well, affirms that it could not last more than one season, because of the poorness of the workmanship. The framework, he says, was nothing but unfinished branches, and the whole thing was so badly done that "la vue seule en fait mal au coeur."[2] Lafitau's statement is perfectly credible, since the Iroquois much preferred the more durable birch bark canoes they bought of the Algonquins, and were not likely to spend much time upon the easily warped elm bark affair of their own manufacture. The canoe was nevertheless one of their most important possessions. Light and easily propelled, it was to the fisherman and the traveller what the snow-shoe was to the hunter.[3] Travelling, in fact, was done as much as possible in the warm season, when the many streams and lakes of the region offered the best of highways, and the canoe the most convenient of vehicles.

To recapitulate:—the production-goods of the Iroquois were primarily such as were needed to aid in the obtaining of raw materials; in other words, they were the implements of special use in hunting or in fishing, or in agriculture: among their possessions was also a stock of secondary production-goods, some of which were used to work up raw materials into finished goods, and others to be of service in transportation.

[1] Morgan, "League," p. 367.

[2] Lafitau, II, 216–217.

[3] The Hurons were such expert canoemen that during the fishing season they often descended the St. Lawrence River to the Gulf. Schoolcraft, "Hist. Ind. Tribes," I, 305.

The consumption-goods of the Iroquois were such as a knowledge of their various productive activities and the nature of their implements would lead us to expect. First and foremost were articles of food. The list included maize preparations, beans and squashes, meat and fish, fruits, nuts, roots, maple syrup and sugar, and non-intoxicating beverages of various sorts. There were many varieties of maize preparations—more than twenty—according to one of the Jesuits.[1] Among the Senecas three kinds of corn were raised; the white flint for hominy, the red for storing—charred or dried—and the white for grinding into flour and making bread.[2] Sagamité, or corn parched in ashes, ground, and boiled with water, formed the standard food of the Iroquois.[3] This "mush" was generally seasoned with dried or fresh fish or meat, with dried fruit,[4] or, for lack of better things, with powdered fish bones[5] or wood-ashes.[6] One of their most delicious preparations was sagamité served in a wooden plate, with two fingers of bear, sunflower, or nut oil poured over.[7] Maple syrup was also eaten with sagamité.[8] Corn meal was also often made into bread. The corn was hulled by boiling in ashes and water. It was then pounded into meal and sifted and made with water into loaves or cakes about one inch thick and six inches in diameter. These cakes were then wrapped in corn husks and baked in the ashes or boiled in water.[9] Maize was also eaten green, roasted in the husk or boiled with beans. Next to maize in the village bill of fare came beans, pumpkins and squashes. Pumpkins were often boiled in water and eaten as a sort of porridge,[10] while squashes were considered especially good when baked in hot ashes.[11] On the hunt and the

[1] Jes. Rel., X, 103.
[2] Morgan, "League," p. 370.
[3] Jes. Rel., XXXVIII, 245; Margry, I, 131.
[4] Jes. Rel., LI, 123.
[5] Sagard, p. 286.
[6] Jes. Rel., XV, 163.
[7] Margry, I, 131.
[8] Lafitau, II, 157–158.
[9] Morgan, "League," pp. 370–372; Lafitau, II, 94.
[10] Margry, I, 123.
[11] Jes. Rel., X, 103.

fishing expedition, meat and fish became the chief basis of subsistence. "It is a savage's supreme good to have fresh meat,"[1] says Father Bruyas. Of that good, however, they tasted only during the three or four months of the hunting season, and occasionally at other times. The surplus product was smoked and dried and taken home to be consumed mainly as seasoning for maize dishes. Several different beverages were in use among the Iroquois. First came water;[2] next came the broth of meat,[3] and even pure oil. There were also two or three different kinds of tea;[4] for instance, the tips of hemlock boughs boiled in water and seasoned with maple sugar, boiled maple sap seasoned with sassafras root, and a drink made of dried fruit with sugar and water. As yet, the Iroquois had not advanced far enough into the agricultural stage to invent an intoxicating drink.

Besides their food for daily consumption, the Iroquois generally had on hand large stores of all kinds, particularly of maize. The latter was preserved in various ways. Green corn was shaved off the cob, baked over the fire in pans or earthen dishes, and dried in the sun.[5] Red corn was often picked when green, and the ears set up on end in a row to roast before a long fire. They were then shelled and dried in the sun. These parched grains, pounded into flour and mixed with maple sugar, formed the main food of warriors on expeditions when hunting and fishing were impossible. Green corn was also boiled in the husk, after which the corn was parched, shelled from the cob, and dried in the sun.[6] This method had especially good results and the product was kept to be made into sagamité for extraordinary occasions. Other grain was harvested when ripe, and the ears, tied in bunches, hung up to dry. When dry enough, the corn was shelled and put away for future use.[7] Corn to be used for seed was left hanging in the cabin. Fish and meat were also stored up for

[1] Jes. Rel., LI, 129.
[2] Jes. Rel., XXXV, 153.
[3] Loskiel, p. 74.
[4] Morgan, "League," p. 330.
[5] Morgan, "League," p. 373; Lafitau, II, 157.
[6] Lafitau, II, 93.
[7] Sagard, p. 283.

use during the year. Drying and smoking were the only means of preservation. In spite of the fact that they possessed find salt springs, the Iroquois do not seem to have made the least use of salt until after their acquaintance with the Europeans.[1] They thought, in fact, that the waters of the springs were poisonous, and that the Europeans got salt from them by a miracle.[2] Besides their stores of fish and meat, the Iroquois also kept quantities of dried raspberries, huckleberries, mulberries, and strawberries, and nuts of various kinds.[3] Finally, animal and vegetable oils were tried out and preserved in lumps or in little round birch bark boxes.[4] All these supplies of grain, meat, fruit, and vegetables were put away in bark cases kept in or near the house, or were buried in caches not far away.[5] Corn was generally preserved by the former method. Packed in bark barrels, it was put on a high scaffolding where it would be safe from moisture, or else in the garrets or vestibules of the houses. Squashes and other vegetables were always buried in bark-lined pits four or five feet deep. There they were perfectly preserved untouched by frost. Smoked meat and fish were generally made up into bundles and wrapped in bark or packed in bark cases, which were hung up in the cabin or buried under the floor near the fire-place. At times, however, cured meat was buried in pits lined with deer-skins. Thus in times of plenty, the Iroquois bill of fare was no mean one. Fresh meat and fish abounded in the hunting season, while in the village, maize dishes seasoned with dried meat or fruits of some sort usually afforded an ample basis of subsistence. In all seasons

[1] Jes. Rel., XLI, p. 125, note 6; X, 101.

Beauchamp, N. Y. St. Mus. Bul., No. 16, p. 75—"Salt they did not use, and it was distasteful to them. The Iroquois now ascribe their degeneracy and lack of manly vigor to using salt meat, instead of obtaining all its fresh juices, as their ancestors did."

[2] Loskiel, pp. 65–66; Beauchamp, N. Y. St. Mus. Bul., No. 32, p. 97; Jes. Rel., XLI, 256.

[3] La Potherie, III, 20; Jes. Rel., II, 123; Bartram, "Observations," p. 73.

[4] La Potherie, III, 19–20; Jes. Rel., XLIII, note 19.

[5] Carr, "Mounds," Sm. Inst. Rep., 1891, p. 516; Lafitau, II, 79–80; Morgan, "League," pp. 372–373; Beauchamp, N. Y. St. Mus. Bul., No. 16, pp. 54–55; Sagard, pp. 250–251.

there was in the village a generous stored surplus to be relied upon in case of need.

Next to food in the list of consumption-goods were clothing and coverings of various sorts. Textiles were rare among the Iroquois. A few manufactures of reeds and corn-husks, bags made of hemp fibre, and some other articles of the sort, exhausted the catalogue. For most of their articles of clothing and many of their mats and hangings, the Iroquois utilized the skins which they secured in hunting. Lafitau describes the dress of the ordinary Iroquois as consisting of about five pieces,—the breech-cloth, the tunic, the leggings, the moccasins, and the robe or blanket.[1] Of these the breech-cloth for the men, and the short petticoat for the women, were considered the only absolutely indispensable garments. The others were worn or not, according as inclination or the weather made them desirable. The tunic was a sort of sleeveless chemise made of two deer skins, fringed at top and bottom. When they were travelling or in very cold weather, the Iroquois often wore a pair of sleeves. These were not attached to the tunic, but were tied together by two thongs which passed behind the shoulders. The leggings were made of a piece of skin, folded and sewed to fit the leg. The Iroquois shoe or moccasin into which the footless stockings were tucked, was also of skin, without sole or heel, but shaped to fit the foot. Sometimes they used for this purpose the skin of the elk's hind leg, cutting it above and below the gambrel joint, and taking it off entire. "As the hind leg of the elk inclines at this point nearly at a right angle, it was naturally adapted to the foot," says Mr. Morgan. "The lower end was sewed firmly with sinew, the upper part secured above the ankle with deer strings."[2] The robe mentioned by Lafitau was a sort of blanket of skins. Upon some of these garments the hair was left untouched, while others had been cured and tanned in the Iroquois way. All sorts of skins were used. One of the favorite sorts was that of the black squirrel. Several of these were sewed together, and a border of tails left along the lower edge of the garment. The

[1] Lafitau, II, pp. 27-31.

[2] Morgan, "League," p. 361.

robe was worn wrapped around the body, and held by the hand or by a belt. A pocket or pouch of skin, suspended from the neck by a leather thong, generally gave the finishing touch to the Iroquois wardrobe.[1] It was, as we have seen, made of materials already secured as a by-product of the food-quest, and though simple was complete and comfortable, and well suited to the climate and occupations of the Iroquois.

The paraphernalia of the Iroquois warrior included some other articles of clothing in the shape of armor.[2] Before the introduction of fire arms, shields were very generally used. Lafitau says that they were made of wicker or bark, covered with skins, though some consisted only of very thick skins. They were of all sizes and forms. Armor, too, was effectively employed to ward off arrows and blows from the axe. Lafitau describes this armor as "a tissue of wood or of little pieces of reed, cut in proportionate lengths, pressed tightly together, woven and interlaced very neatly with little cords made of deer-skin." There were three part to such a suit,—a tunic or coat of mail, leg pieces, and arm pieces. So much, then, for clothing. It remains to inquire what other defenses against weather and hostile beings were possessed by the Iroquois.

The dwellings of the Iroquois, as of nearly all the Forest Indians, were constructed of wood and bark, the most convenient and plentiful material at hand. Even the nomad Algonquins were in the habit of carrying around with them rolls of bark with which they covered the light frame-work of their wigwams.[3] On the hunt and the warpath, the Iroquois used similar temporary structures. In the villages, however, they built large and permanent houses, in which they lived for the greater part of the year. Descriptions of the Iroquois house are many, though unfortunately they are also various.[4] Mr. Morgan's description

[1] Jes. Rel., XLIV, 295.

[2] Lafitau, II, 196–197; Morgan, "League," pp. 362–364; Beauchamp, N. Y. St. Mus. Bul., No. 16, pp. 40–42.

[3] Le Clercq, p. 157 sq.; Jes. Rel., I, 257; V, 27; VII, 35–37.

[4] Lafitau, II, 10–17; Sagard, pp. 250–251; Jes. Rel., VIII, 105, 107; Jes. Rel., XV, 153, 246, note 4; XXXVIII, 247; La Hontan, p. 96; Champlain, "Voyages" (Laverdièrés ed.), p. 562; Morgan, "League," pp. 317 sq.;

taken in connection with the early French accounts, probably gives the best idea of the facts: " The ga-no-sote, or Bark-house, was a simple structure. When single it was about twenty feet by fifteen upon the ground, and from fifteen to twenty feet high. The frame consisted of upright poles firmly set in the ground, usually five upon the sides, and four at the ends, including those at the corners. Upon the forks of these poles, about ten feet from the ground, cross-poles were secured horizontally, to which the rafters, also poles, but more numerous and slender, were adjusted. The rafters were strengthened with transverse poles, and the whole was usually so arranged as to form an arching roof. After the frame was thus completed, it was sided up, and shingled with red elm or ash bark, the rough side out. The bark was flattened and dried, and then cut in the form of boards. To hold these bark boards firmly in their places, another set of poles, corresponding with those in the frame, were placed on the outside, and by means of splints and bark rope fastenings, the boards were secured horizontally between them .... In like manner, the roof was covered with bark boards, smaller in size, with the rough side out, and the grain running up and down; the boards being stitched through and through with fastenings and thus held between the frames of poles, as on the sides. In the centre of the roof was an opening for smoke, the fire being upon the ground in the centre of the house, and the smoke ascending without the guidance of a chimney. At the ends of the house were doors, either of bark hung upon hinges of wood, or of deer or bear skins suspended before the opening; and however long the house, or whatever the number of fires, these were the only entrances. Over one of these doors was cut the tribal (gentile) device of the head of the family. Within, upon two sides, were arranged wide seats, also of bark boards, about two feet from the ground, well supported underneath, and reaching the entire length of the house. Upon these they spread their mats of skins, and also their blankets, using them as seats by day and couches at night. Similar berths were constructed on each side, about five feet above these, and secured to

"Houses and Houselife," pp. 120, 123 sq.; Schoolcraft, IV, 340; Beauchamp, N. Y. St. Mus. Bul., No. 32, p. 24.

the frame of the house, thus furnishing accommodations for the family. Upon cross-poles, near the roof, was hung in bunches, braided together by the husks, their winter supply of corn. Charred and dried corn and beans were generally stored in bark barrels and laid away in corners. Their implements for the chase, domestic utensils, weapons, articles of apparel, and miscellaneous notions, were stowed away, and hung up, wherever an unoccupied place was discovered. A house of this description would accommodate a family of eight." Mr. Morgan is here describing a house for a single family. As a matter of fact, the Iroquois houses were generally built for occupancy by several families. In that case the cabin was made longer by twenty or twenty-five feet for every new fire. The fires were built along the central passage running from one end of the cabin to the other. Each was used by two families, one on each side. A cabin might contain eight or ten fires, and as many as sixteen or twenty families. In the spaces between the platforms, were kept extra mats and cases of provisions. In such a house, Lafitau says, a separate apartment was often left at each end where the young men of the household slept. Passing over one or two details mentioned by Lafitau and omitted by Mr. Morgan, we find that a few rather more important features of the Long-house have been neglected or misunderstood by the latter author. For instance, Mr. Morgan makes no mention of the exterior vestibules built at either end of the cabin. Yet these were important parts of the dwelling, both as places of storage and as general living-rooms in summer. Lafitau says "their exterior vestibule is closed in winter with bark, and serves them for storing their larger fire-wood, but in summer they open it on all sides to get the breeze. During the hot weather, many put their mats on the roofs of these vestibules, which are flat. They sleep thus in the open air, without being troubled by the dew." Morgan seems to be wrong in stating that the upper platform of bark, running along the side of the room, was used as a bed. Lafitau calls this "le ciel du lit," and says that "it takes the place of closets and pantries, where they put in plain sight their dishes and all the little utensils of their menage."

The necessity of defense did not allow the dispersion of the

Iroquois houses, so that each might stand in the centre of its own fields. On the contrary, the settlement took the form of a closely built and irregularly arranged group of from forty to one hundred and forty dwellings of all sizes, the whole surrounded by a trench and pallisade, the latter often supported by an earthen wall.[1] There are many descriptions of the fortified Iroquois town.[2] Lafitau's is perhaps the most complete.[3] "They choose pretty well the site of their villages. They locate them as far as possible, in the centre of some good lands on some little hillock which gives them a view of the surrounding country, for fear of being surprised, and on the bank of some stream which, if it is possible, winds around the spot, and forms, as it were, a natural moat in addition to the fortifications which art can add to a site already well defended by nature. They leave in the centre of their villages a place large enough for public assemblies. The cabins are pretty closely packed together, which exposes them to the continual danger of fire, since they are made of such inflammable material. Their streets are not very regular, each one building where the ground seems most unincumbered and least stony. The most exposed villages are fortified with a palisade from fifteen to twenty feet high, and composed of a triple row of stakes. The middle row is planted straight and perpendicular, the others are crossed and interlaced,—and lined everywhere with large and strong pieces of bark, to a height of ten or twelve feet. Along the inside of this palisade there runs a sort of platform, supported by wooden forks stuck in the ground. Here at fixed intervals they put sentry-boxes, which in time of war they fill with stones to prevent the scaling of the wall, and with water to put out fire. The platform is ascended by means of notched tree trunks, which serve as ladders. The palisade also has openings like battlements.

[1] Jes. Rel., I, 21; VII, 299; XV, 153; Greenhalgh, Doc. Hist. of N. Y., I, 13; Beauchamp, N. Y. St. Mus. Bul., No. 16, p. 11; Carr, "Mounds," Sm. Inst. Rep., 1891, p. 592.

[2] Beauchamp, N. Y. St. Mus. Bul., No. 32, p. 69; Charlevoix, I, 12; Jes. Rel., XXXIV, pp. 123, 250; La Hontan, "Voyages," II, p. 96; Sagard, pp. 79–80; Morgan, "League," pp. 313–314; Carr, "Mounds," Sm. Inst. Rep., 1891, p. 592.

[3] Lafitau, II, 3 sq.

The nature of the site determines the shape of their enclosure. There are some polygons, but the majority are round and elliptical in form. The palisade has but one exit, through a narrow gate cut slanting and closed with cross bars, through which one is forced to pass sideways. They take care also to leave a pretty broad empty space between the palisade and the cabins." Evidently, the village with its large and carefully built houses, and its elaborate fortifications, represented no small part of the wealth of the Iroquois.

The wealth of the Iroquois, then, speaking from the concrete point of view, was a collection of economic goods procured from their environment chiefly by means of hunting, fishing, and agriculture. Of these commodities, a part was valuable as acquisitive capital, either in the obtaining of raw materials, or in working up the latter into finished articles. The nature of these production-goods was directly determined by the peculiarities of the Iroquois environment and by the different productive activities which called them into being. Thus since wood and bone were easy to obtain and to put into the desired shape, these materials were used whenever they could accomplish the purpose in view. Stone, on the other hand, was used only when necessary, as in the manufacture of axes. Since the Iroquois had three chief means of production, they also had three special sets of Primary Production-goods; as, for instance, bows and arrows and traps for hunting, harpoons and nets for fishing, and rakes, digging sticks and hoes for field work. Secondary production-goods were also divided into classes corresponding to the needs of the industry in which they were employed. Thus one set of implements was used in the preparation of food, another in the manufacture of clothing, and a third in the business of transportation. Consumption-goods—food, clothing, and shelter—were all such as could be obtained by a hunting and fishing, and predominantly agricultural people, using the means of production described above. Maize preparations of various sorts were the staple food of the village, and made up the bulk of the stored surplus; but meats and fish were the chief food during the hunting and fishing season, and supplemented maize as a part of the stock laid up for future needs.

5

Undoubtedly field produce formed the larger part of this portion of the wealth of the Iroquois, while the animal world supplied the material of which clothing was made. Dwellings were constructed of wood and bark; those used during the hunting season were small and portable, like the ordinary wigwam of the purely hunting tribe; those of the village, on the other hand, were of the sort characteristic of a settled agricultural people. In other words, the village dwellings were large and permanent houses, carefully built, and surrounded by a strong palisade. All these goods were valuable; *i. e.* they were important to their owners in proportion to the amount of effort involved in their production. As a general thing, the sources of supply were practically unlimited and access to them was free to all. Hence labor cost was the only factor determining value.

Generally speaking, the Iroquois notion of wealth went no farther than the concrete concept from the standpoint of which we have been speaking. Wealth to them meant merely a collection of freely reproducible goods each valuable mainly on account of its usefulness to its owner and its labor cost; nevertheless, the faint beginnings of the phenomenon which Professor Keasbey calls Prestige Value,[1] and the consequent concept of wealth as an abstract fund to be measured in terms of a standard of value, are plainly perceptible. There was one article known to the Iroquois, the amount of which was limited and the value of which was general and social and did not decrease under accumulation; wampum was an object "both lasting and scarce, and so valuable as to be hoarded up."[2] The estimation in which wampum was held was based primarily upon its usefulness as an ornament. Mr. Holmes[3] says that for this purpose "the flinty substances of the shells of mollusks has been a favorite material at all times and with all peoples. Especially is this true of the shell-loving natives of North America among whom shell beads have been in use far back into the prehistoric ages, and who today from Oregon to Florida burden themselves to discomfort with

[1] Keasbey, "Prestige Value," Q. J. Econ., XVII, May, 1903.
[2] Cf. Keasbey, "Prestige Value," Q. J. Econ., XVII, May, 1903.
[3] Holmes, Eth. Rep., 1880–1881, p. 219.

multiple strings of their favorite ornament; and this, too, without any reference to their value as money." . . . "On the necks of brawny and unkempt savages, I have seen necklaces that would not shame a regal wardrobe, and have marvelled at the untaught appreciation of beauty displayed." The Iroquois were not behind the other nations in their love of shell ornaments. Their women and even their men wore necklaces, bracelets, belts, and hair-ornaments made of violet and white shell beads of various sizes and shapes—round, oval, or cylindrical—strung on a fibre or sinew thread.[1] Cut in the form of sticks, it was also worn thrust through the lobes of the ears.[2]

Besides its aesthetic value, however, wampum possessed a certain prestige value based upon the fact that it was not, so far as the Iroquois were concerned, a freely reproducible good. In the first place, the supply was limited to a certain locality, chiefly along the Atlantic coast, to which the Iroquois did not have direct access. Hence the greater part of their wampum had to be obtained in a roundabout way, through the coast tribes who manufactured it. In the second place, even though the Iroquois had possessed an unlimited supply of the raw material close at hand, the prohibitive labor cost involved in cutting out, perforating, and polishing the beads, would have given them a scarcity value.[3] Naturally, the more such ornaments an individual possessed, the greater the prestige he enjoyed. Hence it became an object in itself to be known as the owner of much wampum. Here, at last, was something whose value did not decrease with accumulation. A man could not make use of more than one house or of more than a certain amount of meat or corn, but he could always find a use for wampum. Even after he had decorated everything and everybody that belonged to him, and the utility of his wampum as an

[1] Jes. Rel., XIV, 163; XV, 155, 205; XLIV, 289, 291; Lafitau, II, 59; Beauchamp, N. Y. St. Mus. Bul., No. 41, pp. 326 sq., 356 sq.; Holmes, Eth. Rep., 1880–1881, pp. 230 sq.; Schoolcraft, "Notes on the Iroquois," p. 144.

[2] Jes. Rel., XL, 205.

[3] Woodward, "Wampum," pp. 16 sq.; Beauchamp, N. Y. St. Mus. Bul., pp. 137, 148; No. 41, pp. 330 sq.; Jes. Rel., VIII, Notes, pp. 312 sq.

ornament had sunk to the zero point, still he could lay up the surplus in his cabin, and thereby gain prestige among his poorer neighbors. It is interesting to note how far its prestige value had led the Iroquois and Hurons to regard wampum as the measure of wealth in general. A certain Huron, for instance, mentioned by the Jesuit Relation,[1] returns from a six months' trading journey with his gross receipts entirely in the form of wampum beads, of which he had fourteen thousand. He reckons all his wealth in terms of wampum, and says "that if he were richer" he would give a larger sum to the missionaries. Again, we find a man spoken of as left in deep destitution, "having seen his porcelain collars and all that he had, taken."[2] A wampum collar or belt was as tempting a bribe to the Iroquois or Huron, as a good sized checque is now to the modern politician. It required a stout struggle to refuse it. Thus an honest Huron remarks, "We have nothing so precious as our porcelain collars: if I were to see a score of them glittering before me, to entice me into sin . . . my heart would have loathing for that in which it has so much delighted."[3] On another occasion, a converted woman, transported to the heights of enthusiasm, exclaims "My God . . . I would rather trample under foot a thousand porcelain collars than commit a single sin against you."[4] Finally, we have again and again the direct testimony of the Jesuits that "All the riches of the country" were comprised in the "bracelets, crowns, and all the ornaments worn by the women."[5] True, it is only with the private appropriation of such great natural resources as land and cattle, and the full development of the Proprietary Period that the phenomenon of prestige value and the ability to measure wealth as an abstract fund to be expressed in terms of some unit of value makes its permanent appearance; nevertheless, it was the same principle, working under less favorable circumstances which produced even among the Iroquois a faint prototype of future things.

[1] Jes. Rel., XXXIII, 185.
[2] Jes. Rel., XVI, 205.
Jes. Rel., XX, 223.
Jes. Rel., XXVI, 227.
Jes. Rel., XLII, 155. Cf. VIII, 259, 273; IX, 281; XXXVIII, 271.

CHAPTER V.

THE DISTRIBUTION OF WEALTH.

The system according to which the wealth of the Iroquois was distributed was an exact reflexion of their system of organization for production. Looking from above downward, we find the Confederacy exercising a sort of general control over the whole territorial area occupied by the Iroquois tribes and over that of subject nations. In order to meet necessary expenses, the Confederacy also possessed a treasury of its own, filled by tributes exacted from dependent peoples, and by gifts from the Iroquois tribes themselves. Within the area controlled by the Confederacy, each tribe also occupied its own territorial district,[1] and possessed a treasury of its own, kept full by contributions from various sources. Presents from outsiders and from individual Iroquois who wished to gain influence over the tribe formed one source of supply:[2] the gentes, however, were the chief contributors.[3] The contents of the treasury consisted primarily of wampum. Besides that commodity, the treasury also contained skins, corn meal, meat, and anything else that could be used toward the payment of tribal expenses; as for instance, in the entertainment of ambassadors, and the confirmation of treaties.[4] Captives were, also, sometimes kept as tribal property, instead of being given to some gens.[5]

Within the tribal domain, every one had an equal right to hunt-

[1] La Hontan, "Voyages," II, 175—"Les sauvages se font la guerre au sujet de la chasse ou du passage sur leurs terres, parceque les limites sont réglées, chaque nation connaît les bornes de son païs." Cf. Morgan, "League" (ed. 1901), II, 272–273; Morgan, "Houses and Houselife," p. 79; Schoolcraft, "Hist. Ind. Tribes," I, 278; Margry, V, 395; Jes. Rel., XII, 189.

[2] Jes. Rel., XXIX, 57, 271; X, 235.

[3] Jes. Rel., LVIII, 185, 187.

[4] Lafitau, I, 508.

[5] *Ibid.*, II, 261–262.

ing and fishing privileges and the use of land for cultivation. As regards game rights and fishing stations the distributive unit might be either the individual father of each family, or it might be the men's clan, according as the productive organization was the family or the clan: a single hunter had a right to as much of the produce of his labor as he could carry away.[1] Similarly a solitary fisherman who "has discovered a lake or a good fishing place or a Beaver dam, is owner of it; he marks the place, and no one disputes his right to it."[2] On the other hand, when the hunt or the fishing expedition was carried on by a coöperative group, that group or clan was regarded as the collective owner of the produce. "Each hunting and fishing party," says Mr. Morgan, "made a common stock of the capture."[3] "If they travel in company," says Loskiel,[4] "they have all things in common. They usually appoint one to be their leader, and the young men hunt by the way. If they kill a deer, they bring it to the rendez-vous, lay it down by the fire, and expect that the leader will distribute it among the whole party." Fishing rights were distributed according to a similar plan. Only certain places were suitable for fishing with weirs, nets, and harpoons. Of these natural monopolies, the tribe was the owner, while possessory rights were claimed temporarily by individual clans. In 1753 Zeisburger found between Oneida and Cross Lakes, six weirs owned by the Onondagas. On the Seneca River he went from one to another. At the eastern station he met an Onondaga chief who told him how the country was divided. "It is plain to be seen," he concludes, "that they have much order in their affairs. For instance, each one has his own place where he is permitted to fish, and no one is allowed to invade upon his part."[5] The Oneida annual fishing feast is another good example of the perfect system of clan distribution. "When all were assembled," says Mr. Beauchamp,[6] "a row of stakes was placed across the

[1] Loskiel, p. 78.
[2] La Potherie, III, 33.
[3] Morgan, "Houses and House Life," p. 67.
[4] Loskiel, p. 102.
[5] Cf. Beauchamp, N. Y. St. Mus. Bul., No. 50, p. 297.
[6] Beauchamp, "Iroquois Trail," p. 92.

stream and woven with branches. Then the fish were driven down the Creek, and another row of stakes was placed behind them. When this was done, the spearing commenced, and the division of fish and the feast followed." In the hunting and fishing season, then, either the family or the mens' clan formed the unit of distribution according as the domestic or the clan system of production was adopted. Since, however, we know that the latter method was the more usual among the Iroquois, we are justified in asserting that the clan principle of distribution was predominant even as regards hunting and fishing products.

In treating of cultivated land, Powell and others always speak of the gens as the proprietory group; nevertheless, it must be remembered that not the collection of relatives known as the gens, but only the female members of the kindred group, were the real possessors of the land. The men of the gens had no part at all in the control of the fields from which they derived their vegetable food. Brothers and sons, though just as much members of the gens as are their mothers and sisters, "never have anything but their subsistence," Lafitau tells us,[1] "and have nothing to say as to the distribution of the land and its produce."[2] Understanding the word "gens," as conveying the meaning which Professor Keasbey puts into the term "clan,"[3] we get from Major Powell[4] a very good idea of the general laws of distribution in regard to cultivated land. "Within the area claimed by the tribe," he says, "each gens (clan) occupies a smaller tract for purpose of cultivation. The right of the gens to cultivate a particular tract is a matter settled in the council of the tribe, and the gens may abandon one tract for another only with the consent of the tribe. The women councillors partition the gentile land among the householders, and the household tracts are distinctly marked by them. The ground is repartitioned once in two years. The heads

[1] Lafitau, I, 72–73.
[2] Jes. Rel., LX, 45.
[3] Keasbey, "Inst. of Society," International Mo., I, 355 sq.
[4] Powell, "Wyandot Gov't," Eth. Rep., 1879–1880, p. 65. Cf. Morgan, "League," p. 326; Anc. Soc., pp. 76–77; "Houses and House Life," pp. 66–67; La Potherie, III, 33; Carr, "Mounds," Sm. Inst. Rep., 1891, p. 527.

of the households are responsible for the cultivation of their own tracts, and in case of neglect, the council of the gens calls the responsible parties to account." It seems clear that possessory rights to cultivated land within the tribal area belonged to the women's clans. Within the clan, land was divided among the different households according to their size. In case a family or household moved away to another village, the land which its female members had previously been cultivating simply reverted to the clan, and was disposed of as its officials saw fit. The same general rule that governed the distribution of land and its produce, held good in the case of other immovable possessions,—such as houses. The latter were, in the last resort, the property of the women's clan. Only as a member of the organization did any woman have a right to a compartment in the Longhouse. Thus, while in the hunting season the men's clan tended to be the distributive unit, in the village, on the other hand, it was the women's organization which controlled the surplus and represented the owning class.

To the strength of the clan principle of distribution may also be ascribed the nature of the Iroquois laws of inheritance. Since the individual member of the women's clan possessed only the usufruct of lands, houses, etc., the organization would naturally be her heir. Generally, however, the clan found it convenient to act merely as administrator, giving to the daughter or nearest female relative of the deceased the vacant place in its ranks. Of the personal property of the dead woman,—the implements, cooking utensils, etc., a few were buried with her; the rest went also to her near relatives.[1] Similarly, a man's personal property, his hunting and fishing implements, his clothing, etc., was inherited by the military clan to which he belonged, and was generally given to his nearest male relative in that clan; *i. e.* to his sister's son or his brother. A man's own son belonged to another gens, and hence to another military clan; therefore, he could lay claim to none of the possessions of the deceased.[2] From

[1] Powell, "Wyandot Gov't," Eth. Rep., 1879–'80, p. 65; Chadwick, "People of the Longhouse," p. 57; La Potherie, III, 33; Jes. Rel., LXIII, 183; Lafitau, I, 72–73.

[2] Jes. Rel., XLIV, 305–307.

the point of view of inheritance, then, the clan rather than the organic family, stands out preëminent. The women's clan was the heir of any of its members; the men's clan played the same part in regard to individuals belonging to its ranks. Here we have the solution of the apparently arbitrary custom, according to which women inherited from their mothers, but men from their uncles.

The influence of the clan principle of distribution upon the consumption group is evident in the Iroquois economy. It must be admitted that under almost any circumstances it is not only possible but probable that the family will remain the consumption group. In the domestic and village economy this is inevitably the case. Even in the typical republican and communal clan economies there is nothing to prevent clan members from taking their share of the produce and consuming it in company with their own families and those dependent upon them. Undoubtedly this was often the case among the Iroquois during the hunting season; nevertheless, when no women accompanied the party the men's clan must have consumed as such. Even after the return to the village, the men's clan generally appropriated most of the fresh meat and fish brought back and consumed it in a constant succession of feasts, in which the women had no part. Sometimes, indeed, a benevolent male relative might save his portion for them, but aside from these exceptions, women who stayed in the village were not likely to eat fresh meat from one end of the year to the other.[1] In the ordinary village life, also, the fact that there were two clans—the warriors' and the women's—seems to have had a tendency to cause the consumption group to identify itself with these organizations. The typical Iroquois household was composed not of a husband and wife and their children, but of a group of females, young and old, representing several generations, together with their brothers. In other words, the household or consumption group was made up of a portion or even the whole of a women's clan, and a corresponding portion of the warriors' clan of the same gens. It is interesting to note that the two organiza-

[1] Jes. Rel., XVII, 113; VIII, 143; Beauchamp, "Iroquois Trail," p. 92; Jes. Rel., XV, 183; LXXII, 328.

tions kept separate, even as to the time of eating, " the men eating first and by themselves, and the women and children afterwards and by themselves." Thus even as a consumption group the clan had become prominent among the Iroquois.[1]

It seems impossible that under the communistic regime which has been described, any sort of division into classes of rich and poor could take place. In general, the evidence on the subject tends to substantiate this view. In the Jesuit Relation of 1656, we read: " No hospitals are needed among them, because there are neither mendicants nor paupers as long as there are any rich people among them. Their kindness, humanity and courtesy not only make them liberal with what they have, but cause them to possess hardly anything except in common. A whole village must be without corn before any individual can be obliged to endure privation. They divide the produce of their fisheries equally with all who come; and the only reproach they address to us is our hesitation to send to them oftener for our supply of provisions."[2] In this very quotation, however, there is evidence of some division of the clan into rich and poor. It is " as long as there are any rich people among them " that no one suffers for lack of food. It was indeed quite possible for temporary differences in wealth to spring up between different households; for instance, one family might keep its field cleaner and in better condition than another, and so harvest a larger crop. As long as the other members of the clan had enough to live on, the more diligent might keep their own corn, and perhaps accumulate a large store,[3] adding to it from year to year. This surplus could be expended in feasts, or traded off with foreign tribes for skins or wampum and slaves. Similarly, in the hunting clan, the actual slayer of an animal got the skin as a reward for his skill. Thus a good marksman might come to be the possessor of more skins

[1] Cf. Margry, V, 389; III, 393; Morgan, "Houses and House Life."

[2] Jes. Rel., XLIII, 271–273. Cf. Heckewelder, pp. 268–269. Loskiel, p. 14.

[3] Jes. Rel., VIII, 93–95—A certain rich Huron referred to had two bins of corn holding from at least one hundred to one hundred and twenty bushels.

than the other men. Again, a band of victorious warriors was sometimes presented by the village with a large amount of wampum, which they would divide up among themselves.[1] A skillful gambler, too, could often improve his worldly condition at the expense of his opponent.[2] In many such ways one individual or household might become richer than others, possessing more wampum, clothing, and household furnishings, and entertaining more lavishly. Such differences in wealth, however, were merely temporary. Accumulation, where little beyond vital and aesthetic values prevail, does not proceed far nor last long. About the only object in amassing a surplus was to give it away and so to gain prestige.[3] "You might say," writes a Jesuit missionary, "that all their exertions, their labors, and their trading, concern almost entirely the amassing of some things with which to honor the dead. They have nothing sufficiently precious for this purpose; they lavish robes, axes and porcelain . . . in quantities . . . and yet these are the whole riches of the country. You will see them often in the depth of winter, almost entirely naked, while they have handsome and valuable robes in store that they keep in reserve for the dead."[4] Among the Five Nations, and even among the rather more extravagant Hurons, all this wealth did not go into the grave. Merely the clothes in which it was dressed, a few provisions, and some other little articles, were buried with the corpse. The mass of other things—corn, skins, wampum, etc.—were distributed among the mourning friends and relations, in whose eyes such liberality greatly raised the prestige of the afflicted family. Mr. Hale[5] says that in the latter days of the Iroquois, these funeral usages were discontinued; nevertheless, in its time, the

[1] Jes. Rel., LIV, 25.

[2] Jes. Rel., X, 81, 187.

[3] Morgan, "Houses and Houselife," pp. 455 sq.; Lafitau, II, 89–90; Loskiel, pp. 14, 68; Jes. Rel., LVIII, 185; Beauchamp, N. Y. St. Mus. Bul., No. 41, pp. 357–358.

Cf. A. E. Jenks, "Faith in the Economic Life of the Amerind," Am. Anthrop., N. S., II (1900), p. 683.

[4] Jes. Rel., X, 265–271. Cf. Lafitau, II, 413–415; Jes. Rel., LXXII, 328.

[5] Hale, "Iroquois Book of Rites," in Brinton's "Library of Aboriginal American Lit.," Part II, p. 73.

custom was a good way for a family to utilize its surplus wealth. A similar redistribution was effected by the practice of feast-giving. The feast of Dreams, for instance, was held once a year, or oftener, on different important occasions. This festival, according to one of the Jesuits, " will sometimes last four or five days, during which all is disorder, and no one does more than snatch a hasty meal. All are at liberty to run through the cabins in grotesque attire, both men and women, indicating . . . by signs, or by singing in enigmatical or obscure terms, what they have wished for in their dreams; and this each person tries to divine, offering the thing guessed, however precious it may be, and making a boast of appearing generous on this occasion." [1] Other feasts of a more ordinary character were given all through the year on every imaginable occasion.[2] No one was excluded from these except as a punishment for some offense.[3] The result was that in the long run every clan member was on a level with the rest as far as wealth was concerned. Large public feasts given by one village to another, played the same part in the distributive system of the tribe, as the purely local festivities played in that of the village and clan. In general, we are justified in asserting that the clan was the predominant distribution group of the Iroquois, and that within its ranks control of the surplus was shared equally among the members. Even accidental circumstances making one man richer than another had only a temporary effect, which soon disappeared before the lack of motive for accumulation and the strength of the clan ideal.

Among the rank and file of the Iroquois, equality of opportunity in production resulted in equality in distribution; nevertheless, it must not be forgotten that other classes, outside the clans, shared in the life of the ordinary Iroquois village. These occupied a distinct place in the productive, and hence also in the distributive organization of the community. The monopolistic part in production played by the medicine men gave them a cer-

[1] Jes. Rel., LV, 61.

[2] Jes. Rel., VIII, 127, 143; XVII, 209; XV, 113, 183; XXIII, 187; LXXII, 328; XXIII, 161.

[3] Jes. Rel., XVI, 127.

tain control over the surplus of the clan, which they were not slow to perceive. These people, both men and women, may sometimes have taken part in the productive activities of the clan, and have received their share of the produce; but the main part of their wealth they received in the form of a tax upon the surplus of others, rendered in return for the supposed services of the medicine man in controlling the forces of nature. The medicine man claimed to be able to cure diseases, to bring good or bad weather as he pleased, to make game plenty or scarce, to bring many fish up the streams or to hold them back, to blast or to foster the growth of the corn. No wonder, then, that agriculturists and hunters paid him tribute, and were willing to support him, in order to enlist his valuable services on their side.[1] According to the Jesuit Relations, the Hurons asserted "that the sorcerers ruin them; for if any one has succeeded in an enterprise, if his trading or hunting is successful, immediately these wicked men bewitch him or some members of his family, so that they have to spend it all in doctors and medicines."[2] In fact, it was not unusual for a noted magician to lay a whole country under tribute. Thus in one case a magician exacts gifts from all the villages throughout the region, on pain of non-success in the fishing season.[3] In another instance, he effects the same result by claiming to be able to cure an epidemic.[4] It is not surprising if among the Iroquois, as among the Delawares[5] and other tribes, the medicine-men were the richest people in the country. They formed in reality, a class of parasites living on the surplus produced by others.

[1] Jes. Rel., XVI, 149. Cf. XIX, 83—"Intimidating by their threats those who have not recourse to their art, and on the contrary, giving assurances of powerfully protecting those who acknowledge by some gift the Demon they adore."

X, 199—"The honors and emoluments are always great. These poor people . . . will give their all to anyone who pretends to help them."

[2] Jes. Rel., VIII, 123.

[3] Jes. Rel., XIX, 87.

[4] Jes. Rel., XIII, 237.

[5] Heckewelder, p. 235—"Our doctors are the richest people among us, they have everything they want,—fine clothes to wear, plenty of strings and belts of wampum," etc.

Just as the medicine-men stood above the clan in the distributive system, so the servile classes stood below it. Their part in production we have already mentioned. In the distribution of the utilities they helped to produce, we have the testimony of the Jesuit Relations that they received nothing but "food and shelter in exchange for their ceaseless labor and sweat."[1] Beyond mere sustenance they had no rights of any kind, as long as they remained in the servile class. Rebellion or desertion on their part resulted in nothing but recapture, with cruel torture and death.

To recapitulate:—the system of distribution among the Iroquois is in every respect directly traceable to the peculiarities of their productive organization: within the area covered by the Confederacy each tribe occupied its own territory and owned all the sources of supply contained within the region: within the tribal boundaries the clans controlled the access to the sources of supply; and since the women's clans represented the agricultural laboring force, they also had control of the cultivated land and its produce, and gave support to the warriors only in return for their military services; while, on the other hand, the men's clan was the distributive unit of hunting and fishing life, wherever the domestic economy did not reappear: the clan principle of distribution thus explains the laws of inheritance prevalent among the Iroquois, and also the form which the consumption group tended to adopt: besides the clan, however, there were two other groups to be accounted for in treating of the distributive system of the Iroquois; the jugglers or medicine men, who on the strength of their supposed monopoly in production, received an extra portion of the social surplus; captives and degenerates, who formed a servile class, giving up the whole product of their labor to the clans, and living in a position of absolute dependence upon them. Evidently, the distributive system of the Iroquois is the direct outcome of their organization for production.

[1] Jes. Rel., XLIII, 295.

CHAPTER VI.

EXCHANGE.

The distributive system naturally gave very little opportunity for the development of any system of internal trade:[1] differences in environment and manner of life in different sections of the country, however, led to a certain amount of barter between the Iroquois and other tribes. This trade received a great stimulus after the coming of the Europeans, when the Hurons and Iroquois, thanks to their fine geographical location, took the position of middle-men between the tribes of the interior and the European fur-traders of the coast.[2] With this later development we are not particularly concerned. What interests us is rather the earlier state of aboriginal trade in this quarter. From time immemorial the Iroquois and Hurons had probably bartered their surplus corn and manufactures for the skins and birch-bark canoes offered them by the non-agricultural nomads of the North.[3] The Huron country, in fact, was regarded as "the granary of the Algonquins."[4] With equal truth it might have been called the tobacco field of the region, considering the fact that the Petun or Tobacco nation of the Hurons gained its name as a result of its custom of cultivating large fields of tobacco expressly for purposes of trade.[5] The Hurons and Iroquois also bartered goods with other tribes in their neighborhood.[6] In this way, as well as by force of arms, the Five

[1] La Potherie, III, 33. According to La Potherie there was no internal trade even after the coming of the whites, except in brandy which was sold from house to house by any one who happened to get hold of some.

[2] Jes. Rel., VIII, 57; XIII, 215.

[3] La Potherie, I, 289; Sagard, p. 274; Lafitau, II, 216 sq.; Jes. Rel., VI, 273; XXXVII, 65; XXXVIII, 237; Lafitau, II, 332–333—"Les nations sauvages commercent les unes avec les autres de tout temps. Leur commerce est un pur troc de denrées contre denrées."

[4] Jes. Rel., VIII, 115. Cf. XV, 155; XIII, 249; XXI, 239.

[5] Jes. Rel., I, 22.

[6] Jes. Rel., XV, 155, 247, note 7.

Nations obtained much of their wampum.[1] Most of the finer materials—jasper, white quartz, and chalcedony—used in making arrow-heads, also came from other parts of the country.[2] More or less trade in slaves was also carried on between the Iroquois and other tribes.[3] Charms, too, were objects of barter between the Iroquois and surrounding nations.[4]

The methods by which the interchange of goods was accomplished were those now familiar to all students of primitive society. Among the Hurons, from early spring on through the summer, trading parties left the villages to scatter in every direction among the neighboring tribes.[5] These parties might consist of one or two canoes each holding three or four men, or they might be a large fleet of boats, all travelling together, and filled with traders and their wares and provisions.[6] In the last resort trade seems to have been a matter regulated by the men's clans. According to the Jesuit Relations, a sort of monopoly of the trade carried on at any spot to which he or members of his gens—that is to say, his clan—had paid the first visit, was regarded as a merchant's indispensable right. Similarly the first man to find a particular line of trade profitable enjoyed a certain monopoly of the business, which he shared as a usual thing only with members of his clan, and perhaps with his children. According to the Jesuit Relation, "Several families (gentes) have their own private trades, and he is considered master of one line of trade who was the first to discover it. The children share the rights of their parents in this respect, as do those who bear the same name; no one goes into it without permission, which is given only in

[1] Jes. Rel., XII, 189; L, 135; Woodward, "Wampum," pp. 16 sq.; Lloyd, Morgan's "League" (ed. 1901), Notes, II, 244.

[2] Beauchamp, N. Y. St. Mus. Bul., No. 16, pp. 12–13.

[3] Jes. Rel., XVIII, 173; LIX, 309, note 25—"The Iroquois were habitual stealers and sellers of men."

[4] Jes. Rel., XXXIX, 27; Jes. Rel., X, 51; XIX, 125.

[5] Permission to go was previously obtained from the authorities in order to avoid leaving the village en masse and so depriving it of its garrison. Cf. Sagard, p. 260.

[6] Jes. Rel., XXXVIII, 247; LII, 165; XXXV, 43; XIX, 105; XXII, 75, 81; XXXIII, 215; XXIV, 155.

consideration of presents; he associates with him as many or as few as he wishes."[1] Often the clans combined in order to form a tribal monopoly of certain lines of trade. Father Lalemant says, "The Arendaronons are one of the four nations which compose those whom we call the Hurons; it is the most Eastern Nation of all, and is the one which first encountered the French, and to which in consequence the trade belonged, according to the laws of the country. They could enjoy this alone; nevertheless, they find it good to share it with the other nations."[2]

The chief means employed to bring about the exchange of goods, was present-giving. According to savage custom, any gift outside of the clan involved another in return, and so the desired exchange was effected in the politest way. Thus embassies were often trading parties in disguise. The Jesuit Relation of 1672–3 says that the Iroquois give presents to all the inland natives who visit Lake Superior, "to confirm," they say, "the peace that Onontis made," but rather to get their peltries, with which the Iroquois are expecting these tribes to respond to their presents."[3] Lafitau describes in detail the procedure of the regular merchants upon arriving among the people with whom they wish to trade. "The feasts and dances that the savages give in the course of their trading with other nations make their commerce an agreeable amusement. They pass from one to another as if they were on an embassy. This manner of trading is to proceed by means of presents. Some of them are made to the chief and to the body of the Nation with which commerce is being carried on. It responds with an equivalent, which is always accepted without too close inspection, since this sort of present is perhaps regarded as a sort of customs duty levied on the wares. Afterwards they traffic as individuals from one cabin to another. The thing which is for sale is sent to a cabin, whence in return something else is sent back, which is regarded as the

[1] Jes. Rel., X, 224–226.
[2] Jes. Rel., XX, 19. Cf. XXI, 177.
[3] Jes. Rel., LVII, 22–23. Cf. Jes. Rel., LVII, 23–25; XXII, 291; XXXII, 187; XVI, 129; XLIII, 101; LXVII, 257. Cf. also Bücher, "Entstehung der Volkswirtschaft," pp. 71 sq.

price of the article received. But if the trader is not satisfied, he returns what he has received and takes back his own merchandise, unless something better or more acceptable is offered. The worth of a thing and the desire to have it alone regulate the price."[1]

This sort of commerce was, as Lafitau says, "a pure barter of goods for goods," in which the difference between the marginal utilities of the same good in the eyes of different people caused one commodity to be exchanged for another until each indivdual got rid of his surplus in one line, and supplied his needs in another. No middleman was necessary; there was no market, nor any association of sellers against buyers. There was perceptible, however, the faint beginnings of the development of a circulating medium. That the Indians in their use of wampum made an approach to the money idea is attested by scores of passages from the writings of the early explorers and missionaries. Of the Mohawks, for instance, Cartier says,[2] "The most precious thing they have in all the world they call Esurguy .... Of this they make beads, and use them even as we doe gold and silver, accounting it the preciousest thing in the world." Similar references in which the Iroquois are said to have used wampum as money occur in the accounts of many other writers.[3] Undoubtedly, wampum possessed the necessary features qualifying it for the purpose. Its utility as a source of prestige had already made it to a certain extent a standard of value.[4] This fundamental fact, together with those of the imperishability, divisibility and relatively small bulk of wampum, gave it the place of money in the economy of the Iroquois and of the American Indians in general. Hence, ransoms, fines and debts of any sort could be most acceptably paid through the means of these little shell beads, either counted and woven into strings and belts, or measured out in a

[1] Lafitau, II, 332-333.

[2] Cartier (1535), cit. in Beauchamp, "Iroquois Trail," pp. 114-116.

[3] Holmes, "Art in Shell of Amer. Inds.," Eth. Rep., 1880-1881, pp. 234-240; Beauchamp, N. Y. St. Mus. Bul., No. 41, pp. 351-356; Jes. Rel., XV, 37; LIII, 117.

[4] Cf. Ante, Ch. IV, "Wealth"; Keasbey, "Prestige Value," Q. J. Ec., XVII, May, 1903.

wooden spoon. The latter method was used for small payments.[1] As far back as the accounts go, they give abundant instances of the use of wampum for the purposes and in the manner described. A Mohawk, for instance, mentioned by the Jesuit Relation, came from his own country to that of the western Iroquois to get some beaver skins. He himself had only wampum to offer in exchange.[2] It was, in fact, the common thing to make purchases with wampum, unless something else was specified. Thus among the Hurons, after a year of famine, the value of wampum rose considerably, as they had been obliged to part with most of it in order to buy food.[3] Again, Father Bressani was twice sold as a slave among the Iroquois, and both times was paid for in wampum, the price being three thousand beads the first time, and considerably more the second time. And so instances might be multiplied showing the extent to which wampum money was used by the Iroquois. Undoubtedly in the natural state no concept of exchange value can become prominent, and hence no really important function can be performed by money; nevertheless, in the use of wampum among the Iroquois there can be observed the most primitive workings of principles which dominate the more advanced stages of civilization.

[1] La Potherie, III, 33.
[2] Jes. Rel., XVII, 77.
[3] Jes. Rel., LX, 42-43. Cf. X, 217; XXXIV, 209.

PART II.

CHAPTER I.

THE FAMILY.

From the study of the environment and the consequent productive and distributive systems of the Iroquois, a fairly satisfactory idea has been gained of their economic activities. It remains to examine into their domestic, political, and religious institutions, in order to discover what relation these bear to their economic organization. In the first place, then, what was the form of the Iroquois family?

A general survey of the institution of the family among all primitive peoples in North America shows it existing in two forms. Either the father was its head and the owner of his wife and children; or else the mother took the chief place and added her children to her own gentile group. In the former case the family may be said to have been paternal, in the latter case maternal in character: which of the two forms prevailed seems to have been a matter determined by the industrial organization of the tribe.

In the domestic and village economies there was everything to favor the existence of the small paternal family. The necessity of the preservation of the species allowed the existence of no smaller society, while the nature of the food supply and the consequent method of production encouraged no more extensive organization. For similar reasons the man, and not the woman, was the ruler of the group. True, husband and wife coöperated in obtaining the food supply and in caring for their young; nevertheless, since the woman took a less important part in the food quest, and since the whole group was entirely dependent upon the man for defense, it was in absolute subjection to his authority. The family might come and go wherever food could be most easily found, sometimes congregating with other families in spots where the supply was plentiful, and at other times wandering off by itself alone; always, however, the small family, with the father at its head, was both the production and consumption, and hence also the political unit of society.

In the fully developed economy of the republican clan the family became merely a consumption group, while production was carried on by an organization of men; hence the women and their children were still in economic subjection to the men, and the form of the family was still paternal. Every man was head of his own household, the lord of his wife and children, and absolute sovereign in all domestic affairs. The wife, therefore, left her own people and came to dwell with those of her husband, while the children were added to his family stock and bore his name. The institution of the family as it existed among the Plains Indians, is an example of this type of paternal household.[1]

Under the régime of the communal clan the form of the family changed. Here production was controlled by an organization composed of both men and women. The elevating effect of these conditions upon the position of women in domestic life was at once apparent. The wife was now no longer the humble dependent and chattel of her husband. On the contrary, in every department of social life she regarded herself, if not as his superior, at any rate as his equal. The ideals of family life prevalent in the agricultural communities of the Pueblos and those which reigned in the hunting tribe of the Plains, were, in fact, diametrically opposed to each other. In the latter the father's power was supreme; in the former the mother was the head of the family, owning the dwelling and adding the children to her gens. Thus, while the republican clan economy led to the establishment of the paternal authority; on the other hand, the communal clan economy resulted in the development of the maternal family.

[1] Schoolcraft, "Hist. Ind. Tribes," I, 235, 236; II, 131; V, 183; II, 132—"The husband exercises unbounded authority over the person of his wife."

The disappearance, however, of the paternal group in the agricultural community cannot be accounted for solely by a reference to conditions prevailing at the moment. For since men and women shared control of the surplus, there was no more reason why the mother of the family should have had any more influence over it than had the father. In fact, the fundamental reason for the existence of the maternal family lay in the conditions governing the organization of the community when on the transitional stage between the hunting and the agricultural life. In these circumstances the women's clan, as a result of its monopoly of the increasingly important agricultural surplus, became the dominant power; and hence it was in this stage of progress that the maternal family found its origin. Later, when the full communal clan economy was established, and the influence of men and women was really equal, the women kept the advantage they had gained, and the maternal family still prevailed. A study of the transition stage, in which the simultaneous existence of both paternal and maternal ideals may be observed, as well as the gradual supersedure of the former by the latter, is a convincing proof of the determining influence of economic conditions upon the institution of the family.

Dr. Barton,[1] in his analysis of primitive Semitic life, has made a study of just such a community. Here the women's clan dominated the economic life of the oasis, while the men's clan reached its fullest development in caring for the flocks and in conducting caravans across the desert; hence in the oases the maternal, in the desert the paternal, type of family predominated. An examination of Iroquois society brings to light a somewhat similar state of affairs.

In the Iroquois village, where the women's clan carried on production and controlled the surplus, the maternal family prevailed. "The children," . . . says Lafitau, "belonging to the women who have produced them, are counted as members of the household of the wife, and not of the husband."[2] It was the mother and her relatives who controlled the children, gave them

[1] Barton, "A Sketch of Semitic Origins." See pp. 38–39.
[2] Lafitau, I, 72–73.

names,[1] brought them up, attended to their marriages and funerals, adopted strangers, and, in fact, managed the general life and activities of the household.

Nevertheless, the men's clan was powerful enough to have a decided influence upon the institution of the family. It will be remembered that every gens was subdivided into two clans, the women's and the men's; the one devoting itself to production, the other to defending the gentile group. Now, neither clan could afford to allow any of its members to marry and in so doing to transfer his or her services to any other organization; yet religious scruples forbade marriage between members of the same gens; the result was that marriage became a mere contract between members of different gentes, the bargain involving no obligation to live together; and so the typical Iroquois household consisted of a number of women, their children and their male relatives, all members of the same gens: in other words, the family life of father, mother and children tended to disappear entirely. The overwhelming testimony of both earlier and later witnesses goes to substantiate the assertions just made. According to Lafitau,[3] . . . " the husband and the wife do not leave their families and their cabins to set up a family and a cabin apart. Each remains at home, ... The goods of the husband do not go to the cabin of the wife, where he himself is a stranger." Again in the Jesuit Relation, it is asserted that " their marriages make only the bed common to the husband and wife; each one lives during the day with his or her own relatives. The wife goes to her husband at night, returning early next morning to the home of her mother or of her nearest relative, and the husband does not dare to enter his wife's cabin until she has had some children by him."[4]

The marital relationship was acknowledged, however, by the rendition of certain mutual services. According to Lafitau: " Not only is the wife obliged to furnish food to her husband, to put

[1] Powell, " Wyandot Gov't," Eth. Rep., 1879–1880, p. 64; Morgan, " Anc. Soc.," p. 71.

[2] Jes. Rel., X, 269; Morgan, " Anc. Soc.," p. 84.

[3] Lafitau, I, 261, note 1.

[4] Jes. Rel., XLIII, 265.

up provisions for him when he goes on a journey, either to war or to the chase, or on a trading expedition; but she is also obliged to help her husband's relatives in their field work, and to keep up their fire: for that there are fixed times when she is obliged to have a certain quantity of wood carried to the house."[1] The husband, on the other hand, owed certain duties to his wife: "he is obliged to make her a mat, to repair her cabin, or to build her a new one when the first falls into ruins. The whole produce of his hunting belongs by rights to the household of his wife, the first year of his marriage. The following years he is obliged to share it with her, whether she has remained in the village, or whether she has accompanied him. It is to the honor of the husband that his wife and his children should be well clothed and well kept, and it is for him to see to it."[2]

"The wife's household," Lafitau[3] observes, "got rather the better of the bargain." "According to the common rule, it was considered desirable to marry a girl early; because, besides the fact that the women keep up the family, whose greatest strength lies in the number of the children, the cabin of the woman also profits by the right which the wife acquires over the produce of her husband's hunting. On the other hand, it is not well to hasten on the marriage of the young men, because, before they are married, all the produce of their hunting, all the fruits of their industry, belong by rights to their own cabin. Those of that cabin cannot but lose by their marriage, on account of the new obligations that they contract toward a wife and children whom it is to their credit to support well. And although the cabin of the wife also contracts some obligations in regard to that of the husband, the advantages cannot begin to make compensation for those which the young man brought it before being married. At least that is what I have noticed among the Iroquois." In fact, the advantage was often so decidedly on the side of the woman that the husband even consented to leave his own gens and come to live with his wife. ". . . The mother,"

[1] Lafitau, I, 577.
[2] Lafitau, I, 579–580.
[3] Lafitau, I, 561–562. Cf. Jes. Rel., LXVII, 41; XIV, 235.

says La Potherie, "who knows but too well the advantage of keeping him with her, quietly influences his mind, and it often happens that he never leaves her."[1] In such a case the husband's own clan retained only a formal right to certain military services from him; in all his other activitics he would be likely to be connected more and more surely, as time went on, with his wife's relatives. In short, the advantages on the wife's side of the marital bargain, and the occasional establishment of regular family life, though under the mother as the head, was evidence of the gradual weakening of the men's organization. When the process of absorption of the men's clan by the women's was completed, as it was among the Pueblo Indians, and the full-fledged communal clan came into being, then the ordinary family life reappeared.

The contractual relationship between husband and wife, due to the fact that both were members of powerful organizations economically independent of each other, elevated the position of the wife at least to one of equality with her husband. For one thing, the ordinary form of marriage among the Iroquois was monogamus. Few men would care to take upon themselves the burden of providing more than one woman with meat and skins, while few women would desire to supply fire-wood and corn to more than one husband. Exceptions to the rule sometimes occurred in the families of chiefs. Such men might become polygamists because of their desire to be influential over a large number of relatives and friends. Even chiefs, however, rarely had more than two wives.[2]

In their intercourse with each other, husband and wife were on an equal footing. If they could not agree, nothing was easier than to annul the contract between them. Divorce occurred at the will of either husband or wife. It was usually caused by the failure of one or the other to live up to the obligations involved

[1] La Potherie, III, 13 sq. Cf. Lafitau, I, 577.

[2] Jes. Rel., XLII, 139; Schoolcraft, "Hist. Ind. Tribes," III, 191. Lafitau (I, 155) says that polyandry sometimes occurred among the Senecas. "Il en est, lesquelles ont deux maris, qu'on regarde comme légitimes."

in the marriage contract. If the husband proved to be a poor hunter, or the wife a neglectful provider, the aggrieved party hastened to abandon the one at fault.[1] Each one then resumed temporarily the position of an unmarried person, rendering to his own gentile group the whole product of his economic activities, and receiving from it in return all the services formerly expected from the husband or wife. In early times, especially when the couple had children, divorce was considered a rather discreditable remedy for conjugal infelicity;[2] nevertheless, its possibility undoubtedly led both husband and wife to treat each other with consideration. As a general thing, neither pretended to exercise any real authority over the other, each doing as he pleased in his own particular sphere. The husband, for instance, never seems to have interfered with his wife's management of the children, or the house, or with her disposal of her goods; nor did she, in her turn, meddle in any of her husband's plans for war or hunting. Thus a Mohawk woman, whose husband was urging her to do something contrary to her inclinations, finally replies: "I am my own mistress, I do what I choose; and do thou what thou choosest."[3] Any extraordinary ill-treatment of a wife might lead her to commit suicide, in order to satisfy her outraged dignity.[4] It is no wonder then, that the Iroquois warriors often preferred to marry a captive, rather than one of their own independent country-

[1] Jes. Rel., XXI, 135; XXVIII, 51.

[2] Morgan, "League," 324; La Potherie, III, 13 sq.; Perrot, p. 23.

[3] Jes. Rel., LII, 133.

[4] Jes. Rel., XIV, 37; XXIII, 113-118; XXXVIII, 265; XLIII, 271.

It is interesting to compare the position of the Iroquois wife with that occupied by the married women, for example, among the Domestic and Village Economists of the North, and among the Micmacs of Nova Scotia. Here "the husbands treat their wives very severely; a Frenchman, reproaching one of these savages who was cruelly beating his wife, this barbarian replied that he was master in his own house, and that no one ought to have any protest to make if he beat his dog." (Charlevoix, I, 125.)

Again, the Jesuit Relation refers to the fact of "the men having several wives and abandoning them to others, and the women only serving them as slaves, whom they strike and beat unmercifully, and who dare not complain." (Jes. Rel., I, 173.)

women, since they generally found the former "more obedient and more pliable."[1]

The relationship between parents and children and between children and the gentes of their parents was the logical outcome of the dual clan system. Since children belonged to their mother's gens, their chief allegiance was to this group. They were brought up by their mother and her relatives to be self-respecting members of either the agricultural or the military clan of the maternal gens. The greatest care was taken not to humiliate them by severe or disgraceful punishments.[2] If there was any difference in the value set upon the sexes, it was in favor of the girls. A daughter was, if anything, more prized than a son, because she herself would increase the labor force of the women's clan, and would eventually add her children to the numbers of the gens.[3] From the very first, the Iroquois children were brought up to regard the gentile group as one large family, in which all the males and females of the same generation were looked upon as brothers and sisters: thus within the maternal gens, a child called all children of his own generation brothers or sisters; women of his mother's generation were all of them his mothers; and all men of the same generation were his uncles; his mother's mothers were all his grandmothers; but great-uncles were merely called grandfathers.[4]

The ties between fathers and their children were naturally slight, nevertheless, the relationship was acknowledged in the terminology of kinship, and the rendering by grown sons of occasional military service to the paternal gens. In the latter, a young Iroquois regarded all individuals of his father's generation as his fathers; their sisters as his aunts; and the generation before them as his grandmothers and grandfathers. All young people of his own generation he called his cousins, since they were the children of his aunts; nevertheless, the children of these cousins

[1] "The savages make no difficulty about espousing a stranger and a captive; nay, even, there are some who love them the more, because they are usually more obedient and more pliable." Jes. Rel., XXX, 277.

[2] Jes. Rel., XIV, 37; XXIII, 113-115; XXXVIII, 265; XLIII, 271.

[3] Jes. Rel., XV, 181-183.

[4] Lafitau, I, 552-553; Morgan, "League," pp. 85-86.

[5] Morgan, "League," p. 325; Jes. Rel., XXVI, 297.

would afterwards be reckoned his nephews and nieces, and their descendants would be his grandchildren. After this, the recognition of relationship between members of different gentes would probably cease. Meanwhile, however, the acknowledgment of blood ties between the individual and his father's gens resulted in intercourse of no small economic advantage to both. A father was always ready to come to the aid of a gens to which his children belonged, and a son was expected to be willing to aid his father's relatives in their war-like operations; the result of which was that every Iroquois, though desiring first and foremost the welfare of his own gens, was at the same time interested by ties of relationship in the prosperity of several other gentes. As Mr. Lloyd says: "A Mohawk born of a Turtle father and a Bear mother, would himself be a Bear, but closely allied to the Turtle, and conscious of the blood tie. If he married into the Wolf clan . . . his children would be Wolves. Thus each of the three Mohawk clans would have a claim upon his regard and upon his tomahawk. Whoever might attack, he would fight for his father, his mother and his children."[1]

Quite apart from the family life of the sedentary village stands that characteristic of the hunting or trading expedition. In the village, the influence of the women's clan was predominant: during the hunting season the old conditions of the ordinary forest-hunting tribe were again met with, and social organization changed correspondingly. Husband, wife and children often went off together upon the hunting expedition,[2] and established the regular domestic economy as completely as if nothing else had ever been known. Even when a group of men hunted together as a clan, the old paternal family was likely to reappear as the consumption group. In these circumstances, the authority of the husband was temporarily reëstablished. "The Indians," says Mary Jemison, "are very tenacious of the precedence and supremacy over their wives, and the wives acknowledge it by

[1] Morgan, "League" (Appendix), II, 223 (ed. 1901).

[2] Jes. Rel., LV, 253, 255, 269; Loskiel, pp. 78–79.

[3] "Life of Mary Jemison," pp. 140–141. Cf. Jes. Rel., XXXIII, 109; XXXI, 177, 179.

their actions, with the greates subserviency. It is a rule . . . that a squaw shall not walk before her husband, or take the lead in his business. For this reason, we never see a party on the march, in which squaws are not directly in the rear of their partners." The women's clan, however, was inclined to object to the disintegrating influences of the hunting life, the Iroquois matron frequently refusing to leave the village in order to go into the forest with her husband. In that case, the husband might contract a temporary marriage with some young unattached woman. Such a union lasted only during the hunting or trading season, the couple eventually separating after having divided between them the spoils of the expedition. An arrangement of this kind was by no means an unusual thing. Tailhan speaks of it as a universal custom. According to his statement, "All the savages have wives for hunting trips (femmes de campagne), and also other wives who remain with the rest at home."[1] In this way the hunter sought to solve the problem caused by the conflict between the two productive organizations into which the Iroquois community was divided. But even under these conditions, the existence of the paternal family was made uncertain and difficult by the fact that the "femme de campagne" had no rights of any kind, and on her return to the village was generally despoiled of her share of the surplus by the legal wife of the hunter.[2]

It is evident, then, that economic conditions determined the form of the Iroquois family. In the village, where the women's

[1] Perrot, p. 23, and notes (Tailhan), p. 178.

Cf. La Potherie, III, 13 sq.; Barton, "Semitic Origins," pp. 70–71—"From the beginning there must have been a tendency to the Republican clan. Expeditions into the desert with the flocks in search of pasturage, or caravans from place to place for the purposes of trade, would consist . . . of a considerable number of men and a much smaller number of women . . . . The women of the wealthy Arabians of the oases who to-day accompany their husbands on their expeditions into the desert are as a rule of lower social position. A princess in a harem may have it understood that she is to remain always in the oasis. Probably it was so in ancient times. Such a band of men would take with them some daring young women, who had not much position at home, or who were captives from another tribe."

[2] Lafitau, I, 585.

clan dominated, the family was of the maternal type, the mother acting as its head and having entire control of the children. The strength of the men's clan was great enough usually to cause the marriage relation to take the form of a business contract, involving no common family life together. Frequent exceptions to the rule, however, showed the growing strength of the women's clan in village life. Away from the settlement, the paternal family characteristic of the domestic and the republican clan economy tended to reappear; but the hunting season was short, the wife was often merely a woman engaged for the trip, and no real family life was entered upon. Thus, the ultimate dependence of all upon the corn fields of the village allowed the women's clan to hold in check the men's organization, and to make the maternal family of the village the only one looked upon as regular and legal.

CHAPTER II.

State and Government.

Mr. Morgan, in his books on "Ancient Society" and on the "League of the Iroquois," asserts that the gens is the unit of Iroquois Society. Major Powell says that tribal government in North America is based on kinship.[1] Mr. Lloyd[2] remarks: "The unit of Iroquois Society was not an individual, nor yet a family in one sense of the word, but a household including all the dwellers in one of the communal houses elsewhere described. These households by a process of increase and swarming gave rise to clans (gentes) and phratries, held together by the natural bond of kin. Politically they were united in tribes and confederacies held together by the artificial bond of alliance; but cemented also by the bond of kin. Thus the social organization of the Iroquois was developed through the separation of near kin, and the political organization through the union of remote kin." All the above writers lay stress on the kinship idea. The picture they draw is that of a tribe made up of three or more separate groups of kindred. Though often scattered about in separate villages and hence geographically and economically disunited, each of these gentes is represented as a political unit, composed of individuals of both sexes, each exercising a share in sovereignty on the strength of his or her blood relationship to the other members of the group. A mere study of outward forms, perhaps, might lead to the conclusion reached by Mr. Morgan and his followers; but closer investigation of Iroquois politics reveals certain fundamental peculiarities for which the kinship theory fails to account. Why should the women have exerted any special influence in the Iroquois gens when in similar kindred groups among fishing and hunting tribes they had no

[1] "Wyandot Gov't," Eth. Rep., 1879–1880, p. 68.

[2] Lloyd, Morgan's "League" (ed. 1901), notes, p. 217.

power at all? Why should village have opposed itself to village or tribe acted as a unit against tribe, although each contained fragments of the same gentes? An analysis of the Iroquois state from the point of view of their economic organization leads to the solution of these and other problems of a like nature. It becomes evident that the gens as such was not a political unit: on the contrary, the governmental system of the Iroquois was but another aspect of their organization for directly economic purposes. Not the gentes, but the clans and the villages, represented the fundamental units of Iroquois political life.

An Iroquois village, it will be recalled, was usually made up of several gentile groups, each consisting of two more or less interdependent clans, the women's organization directly controlling the food supply of the group, the men's acting as a sort of standing army for its defense. For military purposes the men's clans were united also into one homogeneous body. This was the fundamental reason for the existence of the village and tribe as economic units. Away from the village, it will also be remembered, during the hunting season, the men's clan alone directed production and controlled the surplus. A knowledge of these facts makes it almost possible to describe by means of the purely deductive principle the organization of the Iroquois state and the form of their government. In the village, it would be expected that the women's and the men's clans would each possess a share in sovereignty corresponding to the extent to which each controlled the sources of supply. Hence the women's clans would naturally be more fully represented in the government than the men's clans: in the hunting season, on the other hand, the men's clans alone would carry on the activities of state and government. As a matter of fact, investigation proves the legitimacy of these *à priori* conclusions.

In the sedentary village the smallest governmental organization was that of the gentile group. So far, Mr. Morgan's analysis is undoubtedly correct. But the gens in the governmental sense was not made up of a number of individuals of both sexes: on the contrary, its constituent units were the two clans, each of which played a distinct part in politics. Each clan had a governmental council of its own, in which were discussed all matters of particular interest to itself. In each gens, too, the old men probably acted as a sort of advisory body, or senate of the clans. Sometimes the councils were attended by every clan member, each one having a right to express his opinion and cast his vote. The conduct of ordinary affairs, however, was left to certain elected representatives.

In the gentile government, the women's clan naturally took the lead. Among the Hurons the Council, though installed only with the consent of both clans, was mainly composed of members of the women's organization, nominated by that body. First of all, four women councillors were chosen by the female heads of the households. "There is no formal election," says Major Powell,[1] "but frequent discussion is had over the matter from time to time, in which a sentiment grows up within the gens and throughout the tribe that in the event of the death of any councillor, a certain person will take her place. In this manner there is usually one, two, or more potential councillors in each gens, who are expected to attend all the meetings of the Council, though they take no part in the deliberations and have no vote. When a woman is installed as councillor, a feast is prepared by the gens to which she belongs, and to this feast all the members of the tribe are invited. The woman is painted and dressed in her best attire, and the sachem of the tribe places upon her head the gentile chaplet of feathers, and announces in a formal manner to the assembled guests, that the woman has been chosen a councillor. The ceremony is followed by feasting and dancing, often continued late into the night."

Among the Five Nations the female councillors of the gens seem to have been three in number.[2] Candidacy for the office of "Oyander,"[3] as these officials were called, was usually a matter of inheritance; that is, the three senior members of a certain

[1] Powell, "Wyandot Gov't," Eth. Rep., 1879–1880, pp. 61–62.

[2] Chadwick, "The People of the Longhouse," p. 36.

[3] "Oyander," Feminine form of word "Royaner," lord or nobleman, the title applied to chiefs. Jes. Rel., LIV, p. 308.

Cf. Chadwick, 39. Cf. Jes. Rel., LVIII, 185; LXIV, 81.

family in the clan were the candidates naturally chosen, unless they were for some reason unfit for the position. The election of these gentile councillors, however, had to be confirmed by the gens and the tribe to which they belonged. An unworthy Oyander ran the risk of deposition. The Jesuit Relations tell of one such case. An Oyander, having become a christian and left her own country in order to dwell in a Jesuit community, was degraded from her noble rank by her incensed constituents, and deprived of her title of Oyander; at the same time another woman was installed in her place.[1]

From among the members of the men's clan, the women councillors nominated a Sachem or Head Chief of the gens.[2] As a matter of fact, the nominee was generally the son or grandson of the dead chief's sister.[3] Birth, however, was no guarantee of election in case the candidate was unfit for the office. Thus, to quote from Le Jeune's narrative.[4] "They reach this degree of honor, partly through succession, partly through election. Their children do not usually succeed them, but properly their nephews and grandsons; and the latter do not even come to the succession of these petty royalties, like the Dauphins of France, or children to the inheritance of their fathers, but only in so far as they have suitable qualifications, and accept the position, and are accepted by the whole country. Some are found who refuse these honors, sometimes because they have not aptitude in speaking or sufficient discretion or patience, sometimes because they like a quiet life."

After the nomination was made, the Hurons required the prospective chief to pass through a period of probation, then, if approved by both clans of the gens and by the rest of the tribe, the election was confirmed and the chief installed by a feast and cere-

[1] Jes. Rel., LIV, 281 sq.

[2] The term "Head Chief" seems preferable to that of "Sachem," the word used by Mr. Morgan. Sachem was an Algonquin title, not used by the Iroquois.

Cf. Lloyd, notes to Morgan's "League" (ed. 1901), II, 217.

[3] Schoolcraft, "Hist. Ind. Tribes," III, 195; Chadwick, "The People of the Longhouse," p. 34 sq.; Lafitau, I, 469 sq.

[4] Jes. Rel., X, 233. Cf. Jes. Rel., XX, 215.

monies similar to those described in the case of the Oyanders.[1] The chief's tenure was simply a matter of good behavior. Bad conduct of any kind, resulting in a loss of confidence on the part of his constituents, was sufficient reason for his deposition by the Council. "The women," says Mr. Wright, "were the great power among the clans (gentes). They did not hesitate, when occasion required, to knock off the horns, as it was technically called, from the head of a chief, and send him back to the ranks of the warriors."[2] Evidently, the governmental machinery of the gens was largely the creation of the women's clan. Out of its own ranks it nominated the councillors; and it nominated and deposed the chief of the gens. On the other hand, the economic interdependence of the two clans was reflected in the fact that the Chief himself was a member of the men's clan, and that neither councillors nor chief could be finally installed without the consent of the warriors.

The functions of the gentile government were largely confined to matters relating to the internal welfare of the gens. The allotment of agricultural lands and the superintendence of the field-labor was one of its main duties. In its keeping, also, was the gentile treasury of wampum, skins, etc., from which were drawn funds for the payment of fines, ransoms, and presents, on behalf of the gens.[3] In cases of crime within the gens, the council frequently sat as a judicial body; and in all transactions with outsiders, it attended to gentile interests.

The hardest worked member of the gentile council was the Head Chief. He was the President of the Council and representative in chief of the two sovereign bodies of the state; hence it was his duty to take the lead in all governmental activities.[4]

[1] Powell, "Wyandot Gov't," Eth. Rep., 1879–1880, p. 62; Lafitau, I, 469 sq.; Morgan, "Anc. Soc.," pp. 72–73; Jes. Rel., X, 235; XVII, note 7; XXVI, 155; XXXVIII, 265; LII, 223; LXIV, 91.

[2] Morgan, "Anc. Soc.," p. 74; Morgan, "Houses and House Life," p. 66.

[3] Lafitau, I, 474–475—"Leur emploi est de veiller plus immédiatement aux interêts de la Nation: d'avoir l'oeil au fisc ou trésor public, de pourvoir à sa conservation et de présider à l'usage qu'on doit faire de ce qui y est contenu." Cf. *ibid.*, I, 506.

[4] Jes. Rel., LV, 55; Morgan, "Anc. Soc.," p. 144.

According to Lafitau,[1] "Although the chiefs have no mark of distinction and of superiority, so that they cannot be distinguished from the crowd by any honors rendered to them, except in special cases, nevertheless a certain respect for them is always felt. It is especially in public affairs that their dignity is displayed. The councils assemble at their summons; they are held in their cabins, unless there is a public cabin destined only for councils, and which is like a town hall; negotiations are carried on in their name; they preside at all sorts of assemblies; they have a considerable portion in the feasts and in general distributions; presents are often made them; and finally, they have certain prerogatives arising out of the preëminence of their position, as also certain onerous duties which serve to counter-balance the feeble advantages that they may have in other respects." Among the "onerous duties" of the Head Chief was the ordering and regulating of public games and feasts for the cure of the sick and other purposes.[2] He saw to it that the poor and helpless of the gens were cared for. In cases of murder, ransoming of captives, etc., he carried on the negotiations between his gens and other tribes or gentes.[4] He was also regarded as the chief custodian of the Public Treasury, from which he drew, on behalf of the gens, whatever was necessary to be munificent.[5] The business of representing the gens in outside affairs was no sinecure. According to Le Jeune,[6] ". . . these positions are servitudes more than anything else. A captain must always make it a point to be, as it were, in the field; if a council is held five or six leagues away for the affairs of the country, winter or summer, whatever the weather, he must go; if there is anything to be made public he must do it."

The political life of the tribe or village was dominated by the same principles that characterized the gentile government. The

[1] Lafitau, I, 474.

[2] Jes. Rel., X, 231; XVII, 201; XXIII, 185, 243; XXVI, 265; XXVIII, 87.

[3] Jes. Rel., LVII, 65; XX, 291.

[4] Jes. Rel., LVII, 63.

[5] Jes. Rel., XXVIII, 87; LVII, 63.

[6] Jes. Rel., X, 233.

tribe, like the gens, was a federation of clans economically dependent upon one another; hence the governmental councils of the tribe were made up of representatives of these bodies. According to Major Powell, the tribal council of the Hurons consisted solely of the aggregated gentile committees and chiefs: thus four-fifths of the council of the Huron tribe were women, while only one-fifth were men.[1] It must be remembered that from the military point of view the Hurons were not so thoroughly organized as were the Iroquois, while agriculture on the other hand was more developed among them than among the Iroquois; hence the influence of the women's clan continued predominant even in the tribal organization of the Hurons. In the Iroquois tribal council, the women were less overwhelmingly in the majority. Mr. Morgan speaks as if the body were composed exclusively of the gentile chiefs.[2] Even if this were true, it would make no great difference in the present analysis, since the Head Chief held office as much by the suffrages of the female clan as of the male organization, and was, in fact, the nominee of the former. Frequent remarks, however, of the old French writers, with many of whose works Mr. Morgan was unacquainted, lead to the belief that the regular Iroquois tribal councils were partially composed of women from among the gentile Oyanders. One of the Jesuit Relations speaks of a Mohawk woman "who by her noble birth is one of the chief women of Annié . . . one of the Otiander, and . . . wont to speak in the Councils."[3] However it might have been among the Hurons, it is certain that among the Iroquois the warrior clans took a direct part in tribal government. In the economic life of the gens, the women's clan played the chief part; consequently in the gentile government the female organization assumed a correspondingly conspicuous rôle. Tribal organization, it must be remembered, brought in several new factors by which the warrior body gained in importance: hence it was but natural that in the tribal council the warriors should have their

[1] Powell, "Wyandot Gov't," Eth. Rep., 1879–1880, p. 61.

[2] Morgan, "Anc. Soc.," pp. 85, 114.

[3] Jes. Rel., LV, 261–263. Cf. XLIII, 299; LIV, 308; LVIII, 185; LXIV, 81. 101.

own special representatives,—namely, the "Common" or "Pine-tree" chiefs. This office was elective and held for life or during good behavior. Ability as a warrior, as an orator, as a councillor, were the qualifications for the position. The number of common chiefs was proportionate to the size of the population, each clan having a certain number. Chiefs of this rank were invested with office by the tribal council, as in the case of Head Chiefs.[1]

Mr. Morgan speaks of these common chiefs as officials, "the very existence of whose office was an anomaly in the oligarchy of the Iroquois." To Mr. Morgan, the gentile kinship theory had to be all sufficient to explain every feature in the political life of the Iroquois, and hence any additional officials outside of the Head Chief and his supporters were difficult to account for. As a result of the subordination of the gentile to the clan hypothesis, it is at once perceived that the gentile council was for the most part the representative of but one of the two clans composing the gens. In the tribal council, it was but natural that the other clan—that of the warriors—should, as a result of their improved organization, at length have insisted upon having its own direct representatives. Hence, so far from being an anomaly, the presence of the Common Chiefs in the governmental body of the tribe seems not only natural, but indeed almost inevitable.

The tribal council of Chiefs and Oyanders, never seems to have taken action on important affairs, without first asking the advice of the Elders of the tribe. The wisdom and experience of these "Old Men" seem to have given them equal authority over both male and female clans. Lafitau speaks of the Elders as a regular governmental body to be compared with the council of Oyanders and Chiefs.[2] "After the Oyanders come the Elders . . .; the number of these Senators is not determined: any one has a right to enter the council to give his vote, when he has attained to that age of maturity to which prudence and wisdom in affairs is attributed as a prerogative, and each one, as is the

[1] Chadwick, "People of the Longhouse," p. 42; Beauchamp, "Iroquois Trail," p. 69; Morgan, "Anc. Soc.," pp. 71–73, 145, 112; Lafitau, I, 476; La Potherie, III, 12–13.

[2] Lafitau, I, 475–476.

case everywhere else, knows how to make himself respected there, according as he has a greater or less degree of astuteness." Lafitau describes in vivid terms the meetings of the Council of Elders. "This council has séances which are private, and others which are public. The former are held to deliberate on their different interests, of whatever nature they may be; and the second to declare publicly what has been resolved, or to discuss all the other affairs of the country which demand some solemnity, such as the reception of ambassadors, responding to them, declaring war, mourning the dead, holding a feast, etc.[1] . . . Those who are to attend the secret council are warned individually; the council fire is always lighted, either in the public cabin, or in that of a chief.[2] . . . Although there is no set time for the holding of these councils, the members ordinarily arrive at night fall . . . . This senate is a troop of dirty fellows, seated on their haunches, crouching like monkeys, with their knees up to their ears, or else lying on their bellies or on their backs; and all of them, pipe in mouth, treat of state affairs with as much sang-froid and gravity as the Spanish Junta. . . . Hardly any one besides the Elders are present at these councils, or have any part in the deliberations. The Chiefs and the Oyanders would be ashamed to open their mouths unless they happened to possess the dignity of age in addition to that of office. If they are present, it is rather to listen and to educate themselves than to speak. Even those chiefs who are the most honored both for their ability and for their age, defer to such an extent to the authority of the senate, that they do not go further than to announce or to have announced the subject to be deliberated upon, after which they always cease to speak, saying, 'Think it over—you other Old Men; you are the masters, do

[1] Cf. Morgan, "Anc. Soc.," p. 18; Jes. Rel., X, 231, 235; XV, 37; XVII, n. 7; XXVI, 155; LII, 223; LVIII, 185 sq.; LXIV, 91.

[2] Cf. References to Hurons; Jes. Rel., XIII, 59; XVIII, 19—"They have in fact no other place of meeting for transacting their affairs than the cabin of some one of the captains." X, 251—"Sometimes this assembly takes place in the midst of the village, if it is summer; and sometimes also in the obscurity of the forest, apart, when affairs demand secrecy. The time is oftener night than day, whole nights often being passed in council."

you order.' . . . The manner of deliberating is characterized by great self-restraint and maturity. Each speaker first restates the proposition in a few words, and gives all the arguments which have been brought forward for or against by those who have spoken first. After that, he expresses his own individual opinion." [1]

According to the usual method of procedure in important matters, the women councillors seem to have met first, and then to have reported the result of their deliberations to the chiefs. "The women," says Lafitau, "are always the first to deliberate or who ought to deliberate, according to their principles, on particular or general affairs. They hold their council apart, and in consequence of their decisions they notify the chiefs of the matters under consideration."[2] Similarly, in matters strictly "de leur compétence," the warriors might hold a preliminary council, and report their decisions to the chiefs. The latter thereupon summoned a council of the Elders, who discussed the matter in secret session, and decided upon some definite course of action. Finally, a great public mass-meeting was often held, at which the whole adult population was present.[3] Here, professional orators from among the councillors or chiefs generally spoke in behalf of the different classes in the village, some for the women, others for the warriors.[4] The Elders were then asked to make the final decision. Thus even in the tribal government, the women's clans took the foremost part, in that they were the initiators of action by the council as a whole. In the subsequent discussion and decision, however, both clans were well represented.

[1] Lafitau, I, 477–481. Cf. Jes. Rel., X, 251 sq.; XV, 27; X, 15—"We pay special attention to the Old Men, insomuch as they are the ones who determine and decide all matters, and everything is ordered by their advice."

[2] Lafitau, I, 477–481. Cf. Jes. Rel., LIV, 281–283—"They hold councils and the Elders decide no important affair without their advice."

[3] Jes. Rel., XLII, 101 sq.; X, 213—". . . although it is the old men who have control there, and upon whose judgment depend the decisions made, yet everyone who wishes may be present, and has the right to express his opinion."

[4] Lafitau, I, 481–484.

Lafitau, in one of the passages quoted above, has given some idea of the ordinary business carried on by the tribal or village council, when acting as a legislative body. According to his account— "all affairs of the country which demand some solemnity, such as the reception of ambassadors, responding to them, declaring war, mourning the dead, holding a feast, etc.," were disposed of by the tribal government. It was its function to deal with all matters of interest to the tribe as over against those which concerned only particular clans and gentes. According to Mr. Morgan, "it devolved upon the council to guard and protect the common interests of the tribe; upon the intelligence and courage of the people, and upon the wisdom and foresight of the council, the prosperity and the existence of the tribe depended. Questions and exigencies were arising . . . which required the existence of all these qualities to meet and manage."[1] Hence "The council of the tribe had power to declare war and make peace, to send and receive embassies and to make alliances,"[2] and to maintain a public Treasury to pay its expenses.[3] In regard to the relations of the community with supernatural powers, it was the duty of the council, under the direction of the medicine-men, to decide upon action and avert disease and disaster, by means of well-timed feasts and propitiatory offerings.[4] It was the function of the council to guard against attack from human enemies, by seeing to it that the village always had a sufficient military force in garrison. Among the trading Hurons the village council always determined the number of young men to go out on trading expeditions and the number to stay at home to defend the village. Sagard says[5] ". . . they do not usually undertake these long journeys without having first obtained permission from the chiefs, who, in a special council, are accustomed to determine yearly the number of men who ought to go from each village in order not to leave them entirely empty of warriors; and whoever should

[1] Morgan, "Anc. Soc.," p. 117.
[2] Lafitau, II, 310 sq.
[3] Lafitau, I, 508; II, 261–262.
[4] Jes. Rel., XVII, 167 sq.; LIII, 275; X, 231.
[5] Sagard, p. 260.

desire to go otherwise, could do it as far as any restraining force was concerned, but he would be blamed, and thought unwise and uncivil"—(*malavisé et incivil*). Similarly, among the Iroquois a war expedition of any size never left the village against the will of the governmental authorities. On the other hand, war was sometimes fomented or agreed upon in cold blood by the councils of two or more tribes, merely in order to keep up the spirit and discipline of the warriors' organization. The most prominent chief of one of the Iroquois tribes forced the unwilling chief of the Neutral Nation to consent to such a war, silencing the complaints of the latter by the indignant query, "with whom, then, he wanted his children to play."[1]

In general, it is evident that the legislative activities of the tribal council were confined to the making of special enactments applying to some particular occasion. Laws, in the strict sense of the term, were not made by the council. In their place, the Iroquois had certain custom-made rules of conduct, looking toward the security of person and property and the general stability of the clan.[2] It was in connection with these fundamental laws that the Iroquois councils became judicial bodies, charged with the duty of investigating and punishing violations of the principles upon which clan life was founded. Murder, theft, adultery, treason, and witchcraft were the chief crimes to be dealt with. In cases where the plaintiff and the accused belonged to different gentes and the councils of these gentes were unable to settle the matter between them, the question came up before the tribal council. The latter then determined upon the guilt or innocence of the defendant, and the amount of indemnity to be paid in case of an unfavorable verdict.

The regular agents employed to see to the carrying out of the legislative and executive decrees of the council were the Head Chiefs of the gentes, who were also councillors.[3] It was their

[1] Lafitau, II, 162 sq.

[2] Powell, "Wyandot Gov't," Eth. Rep., 1879–1880, p. 65.

[3] Mr. Morgan asserts the existence of another set of officials—"The keepers of the Faith." These, besides performing certain religious duties, acted as a sort of police, reporting evil deeds to the council. ("Anc. Soc.," p. 82.)

duty to make formal announcement of the decisions of the council, and to arrange for their execution. Thus it fell to the chiefs to manage the inter-tribal and village games for the cure of the sick and other purposes, and to see to the final payment of indemnities, the settlement of quarrels, etc.[1] Theoretically, every gentile chief was the equal of every other in the tribe from the point of view of authority and dignity; nevertheless, actual superiority in intellect and ability, generally gave some one chief a preëminent position in tribal politics.[2] In foreign negotiations this chief might be regarded as Head Chief of the tribe; his whole nation might even be referred to by his name. To quote from Le Jeune:[3] "There is none [of the chiefs] who by virtue of his election is of higher rank than others. Those hold the first rank who have aquired it by intellectual preëminence, eloquence, free expenditure, courage, and wise conduct. Consequently, the affairs of the village are referred principally to that one of the chiefs who has these qualifications; and the same is true in regard to the affairs of the whole country."

That the chiefs and common councillors were directly representative of the clans, is evident from the fact that in the enforcement of the decrees of the council the chiefs needed no sanction behind them, except that of public opinion. Such statements as the following are frequent in the Jesuit Relations and elsewhere: "They have no government at all; such power as the captains have is little more than that of criers and trumpets."[4] Or again: "There is no government here to make private individuals obey

[1] Jes. Rel., XVII, 201.

[2] Powell, "Wyandot Gov't," Eth. Rep., 1879–1880, p. 62.

[3] Jes. Rel., X, 231. Cf. Lafitau, I, 471—"Quoi que les chefs paraissent avoir un autorité égale, qu'ils soient tous d'une attention extrême à ne pas paraître vouloir attirer à soi les affaires et se rendre despotiques; il y a toujours néanmoins, quelque preëminence des uns sur les autres, et c'est autant que j'en puis juger, ou celui dont la cabane a fondé le village, ou bien celui dont la Tribu [Wolf, Bear or Turtle] est la plus nombreuse, ou bien encore celui qui est le plus considéré par sa capacité. J'avoue pourtant que c'est ce que je ne puis pas bien décider."

Cf. Morgan, "Anc. Soc.," pp. 118–119.

[4] Jes. Rel., XV, 157.

the resolutions of a council."[1] In the Jesuit Relations occur frequent references to councils held to discuss religious topics with the missionaries. It must be remembered that the relationship of the village with supernatural powers was considered as much a thing of public interest as its relationship with other tribes; nevertheless, the decisions of the councils upon these points could never be forced upon a dissenting element in the population.[2] Thus in case the young men proved refractory, persuasion on the part of the Elders was all that could be employed to make them conform to the opinions and decisions of the council. To quote Le Jeune, "In view of the perfect understanding that reigns among them, I am right in maintaining that they are not without laws."[3] It was, indeed, what Le Jeune called "the perfect understanding between them" that gave compelling power to the decrees of the councils. Every individual warrior and every tiller of the fields was so merged in the clan that he could have few or no interests aside from it, and from the gentile body and tribe of which it formed a constituent part. Obviously, any action of his which was contrary to the interests of the organization, was contrary to his own interests, since there was no life for him outside of the clan. The clan and gens, on the other hand, took upon itself all responsibility for the behavior of its individual members. A crime, once proved, had to be atoned for by an indemnity of wampum and skins, etc., paid by the gens of the offender.[4] In case the injured man belonged to another village or tribe than the defendants, the fine fell upon the whole village or tribe of the latter, the one organization thus making amends to the other for the injury it had received in the person of one of its members. "They have only one method of justice for injuries," says the Jesuit Relations, "which is that the whole village must make amends by presents."[5] And again,[6] "The presents given on ac-

[1] LIII, 283, 293. Cf. VI, 15; X, 233, 265; LVII, 67.
[2] LIV, 35. Cf. Schoolcraft, III, 184–185.
[3] Jes. Rel., X, 215.
[4] Jes. Rel., XXXIII, 243.
[5] Jes. Rel., XV, 157.
[6] Jes. Rel., XXII, 291.

count of the death of a man who has been killed are very numerous. . . . It is not usually the assassin who gives them, but his relatives, his village, or his nation, according to the quality or condition of the person who has been put to death." Le Jeune gives a long account of the formalities observed in making amends for crime. His description gives some idea of the trouble a law-breaker caused to the organization to which he belonged. "They punish murderers, thieves, traitors and sorcerers; and in regard to murderers, although they do not preserve the severity of their ancestors towards them, nevertheless the little disorder there is among them in this respect makes me conclude that their procedure is scarcely less efficacious than is the punishment of death elsewhere; for the relatives pursue not only him who has committed the murder, but address themselves to the whole village, which must give satisfaction for it, and furnish, as soon as possible, for this purpose, as many as sixty presents, the least of which must be of value of a new beaver robe. The captain presents them in person, and makes a long harangue at each present that he offers, so that entire days sometimes pass in this ceremony."[1] In short, to quote again from the Jesuit Relations: "The trouble caused by a murderer to an entire community exercises a powerful restraint over them."[2] And again, . . . "their justice is very efficacious for repressing evil . . . for it is the public who make reparation for the offenses of individuals."[3]

Obstinate adherence to a course of action injurious to the general welfare, simply resulted in the expulsion of the offender from his clan and gens. Such outlawry was as formidable a punishment to the Iroquois law-breaker as death could be to the modern white man. The sentence of outlawry was passed by the gentile and tribal councils, and might be of either one of two grades of severity. In one case the man is simply left without the protection of his gens, and his death will be unavenged: in the second case, it becomes the duty of any member of the tribe who meets him, to put him to death.[4] The outlaw generally fled to the woods, and,

[1] Jes. Rel., X, 215, 217.
[2] Jes. Rel., XXII, 291.
[3] XXXIII, 235. Cf. XXVIII, 49; XIX, 85; XXXIII, 229 sq.
[4] Powell, "Wyandot Gov't," Eth. Rep., 1879–1880, pp. 67 and 68.

finding others in the same plight, would cast in his lot with them and make his living mainly by plundering.[1] According to Heckewelder: "Though there are sometimes individuals in a nation who disregard the council and good advice given by the chiefs, yet they do not meet with support so as to be able to oppose the measures of government. They are generally looked upon as depraved beings who, not daring to associate with the others, lurk about by themselves, generally bent on mischief of a minor kind, such as pilfering small articles of goods and provisions. As soon, however, as they go a step further, and become known thieves and murderers, they are considered a disgrace to the nation, and being in a manner disowned by it, they are no longer entitled to its protection."[2]

Heckewelder goes on to give an instance of outlawry met with by him among the Senecas:[3] "When in the winter of 1788 and 1789, the Indian Nations were assembling at Fort Harmer . . . where a treaty was to be held, an Indian of the Seneca Nation was one morning found dead on the bank of the river. The Cornplanter, chief of this nation, observing some uneasiness among the officers and people of the place, and fearing the murder might create undue disturbance, waited in the morning on the governor, whom he desired 'not to be uneasy about what had happened the preceding night, for the man who had been killed was of no consequence,' which statement meant that he was disowned for his bad conduct by his countrymen, and that his death would not be a loss to his nation."

While ordinary manifestations of a non-social spirit led to the exclusion of the culprit from the ranks of the clan, direct treason resulted in his immediate execution. Treason consisted in revealing the secrets of medicine preparations supposed to bring good fortune, or in giving any other information or assistance to enemies of the tribe. The criminal was tried before the tribal council, and if convicted, was put to death on the spot.[4] Such a

[1] Loskiel, pp. 102–103.
[2] Heckewelder, p. 111.
[3] *Ibid.*, p. 112.
[4] Powell, "Wyandot Gov't," Eth. Rep., 1879–1880, p. 67.

person was too dangerous to society to be permitted to live, even as an outlaw. Witchcraft, the injury of anyone by supernatural means, was regarded as only a more terrible form of treason.[1]

Tribal government, then, was not merely a question of the orderly living together of several sets of relatives; it was rather a system regulating the life of a large economic group composed of many smaller organizations of the same sort. It was, in fact, a machine created by the women's and men's clans, and controlled by each exactly in proportion to the amount of influence exerted by each in economic life. Created and operated by the clans themselves, with a view to their own prosperity, the system needed no sanction beyond public opinion.

The government of the confederacy embodied simply a repetition of the principles animating gentile and tribal life; in other words, it was representative of the clans of the whole country of the Iroquois acting in unison. For this purpose they had been grouped in villages and in tribes, and now these latter bodies were gathered together in one great nation. The governmental activities of the confederacy were carried on by a council consisting of the gentile chiefs of all the different tribes.[2] Their number, at first fifty, was afterwards but forty-eight, since two places of the original fifty were filled but once. A certain name was attached to each office, and during his term of service each incumbent was known by this instead of his own name. In a sense, therefore, the officials of the confederacy never died. Just as the gentes and the tribes were immortal, so also were those who represented them in the government of the confederacy. Of the fifty chieftainships, there were nine among the Mohawks, nine among the Oneidas, fourteen among the Onondagas, ten among the Cayugas and eight among the Senecas. There were three chiefs from each

[1] See note 1. Cf. Jes. Rel., LXII, 99; Morgan, "League," p. 330; Jes. Rel., X, 223—"They also punish sorcerers severely, that is, those who use poisoning and cause death by charms; and this punishment is authorized by the consent of the whole country, so that whoever takes them in the act has full right to cleave their skulls—without fear of being called to account."

[2] Cf. Morgan, "Anc. Soc.," Ch. 5; Schoolcraft, "Hist. Ind. Tribes," III, 186; Chadwick, "People of the Longhouse," p. 33.

of the Mohawk gens, and the same from the Oneidas: the Senecas, on the other hand, had eight gentes, not all of whom were represented in the council. The unrepresented gentes, however, were probably small and unimportant offshoots of older bodies. The same state of affairs is found in the other Iroquois tribes.

In council, the chiefs voted by tribes, each tribe exercising the same amount of power as any other, even though it may have had a smaller number of representatives. Unanimity was necessary for a decision. This was generally achieved through a system of voting in classes. The exact principle upon which the classes were arranged is not clear. In all probability the matter was decided upon the basis of locality; that is, if a tribe had three villages, the chiefs in each village would form a class, and vote as one man.[1] Hence the final problem would involve only the agreement of three votes in order to allow the tribe to vote as a unanimous whole. It is obvious that by this system two Bear chiefs, for instance, living in different villages, might find themselves voting in different classes. Now if the gens, in the sense of a family stock, was really the unit of Iroquois politics, this would be impossible. Instead of voting by villages, the chiefs would have voted according to their gentes, all the Bears voting together, and so on. The chief was really the representative of the clan and the village, and hence was for all practical purposes more closely allied with the Wolf and Turtle chief of his own village, than with other chiefs of the same family stock, but of a different town. The method of voting in the council of the confederacy, therefore, forms only one more proof of the fact that not merely blood relationship, but also, and primarily, common economic interests formed the tie that bound the Iroquois into a society.[2]

[1] Cf. Lloyd, Appendix to Morgan's "League" (ed. 1901), p. 215—"The division of the sachems of each tribe into classes, probably represents the original division of the tribe into villages."

[2] The Seneca Tribe voted in four classes:—Class I: Turtle chief and Snipe chief. Class II: Turtle chief and Hawk chief. Class III: Bear chief and Snipe chief. Class IV: Snipe chief and Wolf chief.

Cf. Morgan, "Anc. Soc.," p. 131.

Besides the chiefs and their aids,[1] any other clansman or woman could come to the council and express his or her opinion. In the confederacy, as in the gens, state and government were kept in close contact. Often, if the case was an important one, nearly the whole population of all the villages from near and far would flock to the council meeting. There, for the sake of convenience, women and warriors, chiefs and old men, would often hold their separate councils; and eventually, through appointed orators, express their opinions before the council of the confederacy, with whom lay the power of final decision.[2]

The council met regularly once a year at Onondaga, a central point, and regarded as the capital of the confederacy.[3] It could be summoned at any other time by any one of the tribes. In that case, the tribe in question fixed the date and place of meeting.[4]

The functions of the council were twofold. In the first place, it saw to it that the internal affairs of the confederacy were in good order; it settled quarrels between the different tribes, invested chiefs with office, etc.: in the second place, it attended to the foreign relations of the confederacy; and so deliberated upon war and peace, sent and received embassies, and attended to the affairs of subjugated tribes[5]

[1] Morgan, "Anc. Soc.," 131–132. "Each sachem had an assistant sachem, who was elected by the gens of his principal from among its members, and who was installed with the same forms and ceremonies. He was styled an aid. It was his duty to stand behind his superior on all occasions of ceremony, to act as his messenger, and in general to be subject to his directions. It gave to the aid the office of chief, and rendered probable his election as the successor of his principal after the decease of the latter."

[2] Parkman, "Jesuits in North America," p. lix; Morgan, "Anc. Soc.," p. 128.

[3] Jes. Rel., LI, 237; Morgan, "Anc. Soc.," pp. 128, 135.

[4] Lloyd, Morgan's "League" (ed. 1901), II, 244–245; The Huron council met in same manner at Ossossané. Jes. Rel., V, n. 60, p. 259, 261; XIII, 37.

[5] Morgan, "Anc. Soc.," pp. 133, 142–143. Beauchamp, N. Y. St. Mus. Bul., No. 41, p. 383. Cf. Colden, "History of the Five Nations," p. 3: "All the nations round them have for many years entirely submitted to them, and pay a yearly tribute to them in wampum; they dare neither

The confederacy, like the Tribe, had no particular machinery for executing its decisions. Anything decreed by the council would be carried out by special agents appointed for the purpose, or by each tribe as it saw fit. Certain duties were fulfilled by certain tribes. Thus one of the Onondaga councillors was the keeper and interpreter of the wampum records, while the Mohawks saw to the collection of tribute from subject tribes. There was no chief executive magistrate of the confederacy, since no member of the council could claim any higher rank than any other. If one were better known than another, it was not on account of any official distinction, but merely on account of superior ability, or fitness to represent the nation in some special transaction.[1]

So far, the subject under discussion has been the government of the sedentary community, as a whole. It must not be forgotten, however, that, for a large portion of the year, the men's clans led a life quite apart from the life of the village, and even while there, they regarded themselves as more or less transient sojourners; hence, the warriors had a government of their own, distinct from that of the women's clans, and of the sedentary community in which the influence of the latter tended to predominate. Among the Hurons, according to Major Powell, the military government was completely differentiated from the civil.[2] The former inhered in a military chief, and in a council composed of all the able-bodied warriors of the tribe. All councils of war were held in the cabin of the "great war captain," and condemned

make war nor peace without the consent of the Mohawks. Two Old Men commonly go about every year or two to receive this tribute. . . . It is not for the sake of tribute, however, that they make war, but from the notions of glory which they have ever most strongly imprinted on their minds."

Cf. Jes. Rel., XXXI, 89; XXXVI, 105; Chadwick, "People of the Longhouse," p. 76; Beauchamp, N. Y. St. Mus. Bul., No. 41, p. 457; Schoolcraft, "Hist. Ind. Tribes," III, 185; Woodward, "Wampum," pp. 16 sq.; Morgan, "Anc. Soc.," p. 149; Heckewelder, pp. 56–57, 59, n. 3; Carr, "Mounds," Sm. Inst. Rep., 1891, pp. 518, 522.

[1] Morgan, "Anc. Soc.," pp. 128, 145; Jes. Rel., X, 231; XII, 53.

[2] Powell, "Wyandot Gov't," Eth. Rep., 1879–1880, p. 61.

captives were tortured there.[1] Among the Iroquois, says Lafitau, "The warriors have also a separate council for matters which are in their line."[2] The commander-in-chief of the warriors was nominally the Head Chief of the gens. Lafitau says, "The chiefs of the gentes are ordinarily at their head, when they have given proof of prowess in military affairs, and when they are capable of taking command."[3] Nevertheless, the Head Chiefs were, as a usual thing, only the connecting link between the warriors' and the women's clans. Practically, the former recognized as military chiefs those who rendered themselves worthy of the position, being conspicuous for feats of valor, for good conduct, and service. Before the formation of the confederacy, at any rate, no man was recognized as the war chief par excellence, though the common chiefs, who took part in the tribal council, were generally recognized to be conspicuous military leaders.[4] Cusick says that after the formation of the confederacy, when a war was undertaken which involved the whole country, the Bear clans selected the "Great Warrior" or commander.[5] Mr. Morgan says that there were two permanent war chiefs of the confederacy; one selected from the Wolf, the other from the Turtle Clan of the Senecas.[6] In general, however, Mr. Morgan further says that[7] "Military operations were usually left to the action of the voluntary principle. . . . Any person was at liberty to organize a war party and conduct an expedition wherever he pleased. He announced his project by giving a war dance and inviting volunteers. This method furnished a practical test of the popularity of the undertaking. If he succeeded in forming a company, which would consist of such persons as joined him in the dance, they departed immediately, while enthusiasm was at its height. When a tribe was menaced with an attack, war parties were formed to meet it in much the same manner. When forces thus raised

[1] Jes. Rel., XIII, 59.
[2] Lafitau, I, 476.
[3] *Ibid.*, pp. 477–481.
[4] Morgan, "League," p. 72–74.
[5] Chadwick, "People of the Longhouse," p. 43.
[6] Morgan, "Anc. Soc.," pp. 146–147.
[7] *Ibid.*, pp. 117–118.

were united in one body, each was under its own war-captain, and their joint movements were determined by a council of these captains. If there was among them a war chief of established reputation, he would naturally become their leader." Once made up, a war party, whether enlisted for a few days or for several years, formed a most rigid organization. Obedience to their chosen leaders was absolute, and desertion was punished by death.[1]

On the hunting expedition, the same principle prevailed as upon the warpath. The men's clan in each case was the sovereign body. Government was carried on by a council of the hunters. If any leader was needed, he was chosen for his merits as a hunter. Women, if they accompanied the party, were entirely subordinate to the men.

Evidently, the government of the Iroquois was a government for and by the clans, acting in an assembly composed either of representatives or of all the members of a clan. The latter was so often the case that according to Mr. Morgan:[2] "It may be said that the life of the Iroquois was either spent in the chase, on the war path, or at the council-fire. They formed the three leading objects of his existence, and it would be difficult to determine for which he possessed the strongest predilection." "Practically considered," says Schoolcraft, "a purer democracy perhaps never existed. The chiefs themselves had no power in advance of public sentiment."[3]

The conception of absolute sovereignty resting in the clans need be disturbed in no way by the fact that some authorities speak frequently of the existence of an aristocracy among the Iroquois. Lafitau, for instance, speaks of the order of the "'Qesendouáns,' that is to say, noble families."[4] A Jesuit chronicler says, too, that "they have the nobility here as well as in France, and are as proud of it . . . ."[5] Again, we find mention of a woman "who

[1] Lafitau, II, 162.
[2] Morgan, "League," 107-108.
[3] Schoolcraft, "Notes on the Iroquois," p. 84.
[4] Lafitau, I, 563.
[5] Jes. Rel., XXVI, 307.

by her noble birth is one of the chief women of Annié . . . one of those who are noble and of high station."[1] The "nobility" here spoken of were, in fact, only the governmental officials of the clans. The offices of chief and councillor, it will be remembered, were usually occupied by members of some particular family. These people inherited office, however, only in the sense that their birth made them *ipso facto* candidates, but their candidacy had to be approved by the clans and confirmed by an election: before that occurred, their position in the community in no way differed from that of any other member of a clan.

Nevertheless, the Iroquois village was by no means so complete a democracy as Mr. Morgan and others like to picture it. In every Iroquois tribe, a large part of the population was practically disfranchised. It has been shown that sovereignty was in the hands of the clan organization. Now, though every one in the village was associated with some gens, not everyone was a member in full standing of either the male or the female clan of that gens. On the contrary, in every gentile group there were always numbers of captives who, though destined perhaps to full membership in one of the clans, were as yet still in the slave status. About 1680, within a year or two, thirteen hundred such captives were brought in from neighboring tribes.[2] Most of these additions to the population were boys and young women and girls. They were given to such gentes as wished to increase their numbers, and in future were regarded as belonging to that particular group, rather as chattels, however, than as members of the organization.[3] The position of these captives was, for a time at least, not at all enviable. The gens to which they belonged would probably protect them from injury from outsiders, but within the gens there was absolutely nothing to guarantee their safety. Possessing no voice in council, and no rights of any kind, they spent their whole time producing for the benefit of their masters. In return they received food and shelter as long as they were capable,

[1] Jes. Rel., LV, 261–263. Cf. XLIII, 299; LVIII, 185.

[2] Jes. Rel., LXII, 71; XXXVI, 177; XXXIX, 219.

[3] Jes. Rel., XXXI, 53; XXIV, 285.

healthy, and obedient. An unskillful slave was sold for a song,[1] and a sick slave was either abandoned or killed outright.[2] The least cause of irritation often resulted in the death punishment. Young women slaves especially were "constantly exposed to danger through the brutal lechery or cruelty of their masters or mistresses .... The only punishment for even their slightest faults is death," says a Jesuit chronicler.[3] Yet if she escaped all these dangers, a young female captive might in the end hope to marry an Iroquois, and become a matron of equal standing with any other. Similarly, a male captive, after the death of his first owners, might become a freeman, might marry and have children, and in case of great ability, might even become a leader in the community. The Jesuit Relations mention one instance of the latter sort, when speaking of a man "formerly a captive of the Iroquois, and now a captain among them."[4] Just what was the final status of the ordinary captive blessed with no marked ability, is a question hard to decide. Testimony rather goes to show that he never became a clansman in the full sense of the word, since he was never allowed to vote in the council.[5] If this is so, then the number of disfranchised among the Iroquois must have been comparatively large. It must be remembered, too, that captive slaves were not the only individuals in an Iroquois village who possessed no share in sovereignty. With the captives must be classed all males who through laziness or some other infirmity of body or of will had fallen out of the warriors' organization

[1] Father Bressani says that he was sold cheap (3,000 porcelain beads), because of his lack of skill as a laborer and his ailments. Jes. Rel., XXXIX, 77.

[2] Jes. Rel., XLIII, 303.

[3] Jes. Rel., XLIII, 295. Cf. XLII, 137; XLIII, 299; XLIII, 295—"When a Barbarian splits the head of his slave with a hatchet, they say: 'It is a dead dog; there is nothing to be done but to cast it upon the dunghill.'"

[4] Jes. Rel., XLII, 57.

[5] Jes. Rel., XLIII, 293: "... those who, having willingly submitted to the yoke of the conquerors ... have become heads of families after the death of their masters, or have married. Although they lead a tolerably easy life, they are looked upon as slaves and have no voice, either active or passive, in the public councils."

and taken to doing women's work. These effeminate men were not received into the women's clan, but were merely classed with the slaves, and not permitted to exercise the right of suffrage.[1] A sort of temporary slavery was sometimes the fate of the unsuccessful gambler. A man might stake his freedom for two or three years, during which time the other party in the game employed him as a servant. Such a slave was generally well treated and set free again at the end of his term.[2]

It is clear that all that large portion of the Iroquois population which was debarred from free access to the social surplus, a privilege controlled by clans of which they were not members, were at the same time, *ipso facto,* kept " without the state." They were a disfranchised class having no share of sovereign power, and no voice in the government of the group to which they belonged. The fact that they were gentiles made no difference in their lot: the essential fact was that they were not members of clans. The clan, then, and not the gens as such seems to have been the political unit in the Iroquois village; that is to say, economic conditions, rather than ties of kinship or religion, decided the form of state and government among the Iroquois.

The position of the Jugglers or Medicine-men in the community, strengthens the hypothesis just stated. These men controlled the access to the supernatural powers without whose favor no activities of the clans could succeed in their purpose; hence, it will be remembered,[3] the Jugglers were able to form a separate income class, taking from the clans a part of their surplus; hence, also, they controlled political life to a certain extent, and were able to force their decisions upon the clans. According to the Jesuit Relations, it was " the highest duty of the Captains to obey these impostors."[4]

[1] Jes. Rel., XLIII, 293; LVII, 85; Carr, "Mounds," Sm. Inst. Rep., 1891, p. 517.

[2] Jes. Rel., XVI, 201.

[3] Cf. Ante, Distribution.

[4] Jes. Rel., XXIII, 45; XXX, 205.

CHAPTER III.

RELIGION.

In the religious systems of all primitive peoples the influence of their economic life is extremely apparent. The nature and relative authority of their deities, the ceremonials of their worship, and the organization of the worshippers, may in nearly every case be considered the direct consequents of certain economic antecedents. The savage always deifies the most conspicuous sources, direct or indirect, from which he derives his supply of economic goods, and worships these divinities with ceremonies appropriate to their nature. Moreover, the form of organization of any given people for purposes of worship, generally corresponds to their organization for purposes of production. In a word, the main features of the religious system of any society, as Professor Keasbey ably argues, are determined largely by the manner and by the method of production characteristic of their economy.

The manner of production usual in the barren and jungle environment gives rise to the lowest form of religious development, —a simple Fetishism. Here the nature of the food supply, at once so heterogeneous and so scanty, offers but small opportunity for the growth of the powers of observation and classification. The savage regards everything in nature as possessing intelligence, and therefore able to help or hinder him in his struggle for existence; hence the little family group, wandering perpetually from place to place, and dependent for subsistence on whatever it can find, simply tries to propitiate anything and everything in its immediate environment which might increase or diminish its food supply. Such a group has but little idea of any deities outside of the material objects to be seen around them, or of any specific forms of worship. Similarly, as there is no coöperation in production, so also there is none for purposes of worship. In the conditions giving rise to the domestic economy, no organization outside of the small family is possible or desirable. Inevitably then, the religious life is carried on after the same manner, each individual having his own charms for luck, and performing whatever rites he may think advisable, at whatever time and place he wishes. The religion of the domestic economist, then, is characterized by a promiscuous fetishism, by little or no development of ceremonial, and by a purely individual, or at most family, system of worship.

Among more favorably situated hunting or pastoral tribes fetishism by no means entirely disappears; at the same time new and better conditions cause an advance in religious ideas. The life of the primitive hunter or herder is far less hap-hazard and hand to mouth than that of the inhabitant of the desert or the jungle. The former is able to depend for food-supply on one or two great, and more or less reliable sources,—cattle, perhaps, as in the Old World, or the animals of the chase, as in North America.[1] These conditions tend to reduce the diversity of the powers to be propitiated. Instead of worshipping everything around him, he confines his attention to animals and to whatever forces of nature hinder or help him in his pursuit or care of them. The hunter or herder, however, is not likely to worship individual animals. The homogeneity of his food supply develops to some extent the savage's power of classifying and abstracting. He therefore conceives the idea of a type to which individual members of a species conform; hence the type rather than the individual becomes the real object of worship.[2]

[1] The Plains tribes of the United States looked to the buffalo, and the eastern Indians to the deer, bear, and other forest animals, as the chief means of satisfying their wants.

[2] The herder of the Old World proceeded somewhat further, worshipping not so much the type of the animal, as the procreative force which kept up his herd. The North American hunter, however, who lived on wild animals with the preservation of whose species he had nothing to do, was content with the more primitive conception; accordingly he imagined that each animal species was typified by some great progenitor or Elder Brother, and remained under this mysterious being's care. It was primarily to the latter that the Indian addressed his prayers and sacrifices; while he re-

As to ceremonial observances, any mention of the rites of the herder—since pastoral life was unknown in North America—may be omitted and only those customary in hunting tribes considered. Among the latter, ceremonials of worship, though still of the simplest kind, are somewhat more regular and definite than those among the inhabitants of barren and jungle regions. Just as there is an increasing clearness in ideas of the deities, so there is manifest a corresponding development in the forms by which these supernatural powers are propitiated.

In the republican clan economy, access to the surplus is controlled mainly by the clan rather than the individual; hence the group, as such, offers prayers and sacrifices to propitiate whatever powers have influence upon its welfare. In other words, not the individual member, but the clan as a whole, under its regular leaders, attends personally to the religious rites and ceremonies deemed necessary to keep the powers in good humor. From the very nature of hunting life, no priestly intervention is needed between the clan and its gods. Ceremonies, though frequent, are not elaborate enough to confuse any clan member; furthermore, in the hunting life, no special class of learned men is needed to direct the activities of the clan: hence no set of men, on the strength of superior knowledge of this sort, can assume authority over the rest and so become the priestly class of the community. In the hunting life, then, organization for purposes of worship is identical with that formed for production.

Nevertheless, the existence of jugglers or medicine-men must not be ignored. In the worship of the deities, it is true, no priestly class has as yet arisen. On the other hand, the clan does not pretend to have any special means of communicating with supernatural beings, or of finding out their will; this task is left to the jugglers, each one of whom claims to have some special friend among the gods over whom he has influence; and hence these men in the last resort, by controlling the clan's access to the surplus, form a class above the clan, and gain great power over it.

In the typical agricultural community, a difference in manner

garded individual animals merely as intelligent beings on a par with himself.

and a development in method of production cause a corresponding change in religious life. Plants and vegetables are now the chief source of the surplus; therefore plant, rather than animal deities are characteristic of agricultural polytheism. Moreover, the opportunity of the agriculturist to observe the phenomena of production and growth causes an exaltation of the idea of fertility: hence as the herder of the Old World worshipped the procreative power that kept up his herd, so the agriculturist adores the productive and rejuvenating force that gives him his yearly crop of corn. At the same time, the extremely close relation between climatic conditions and vegetable life causes the primitive agriculturist to feel the deepest veneration for atmospheric phenomena, and consequently his conceptions of the weather gods become much clearer and more definite than those of the hunter.

The fact that agricultural operations are carried on in regular succession at certain fixed seasons of the year causes a corresponding regularity and fixedness in the performance of religious rites and ceremonies. It is in spring and fall, the seasons of planting and harvesting, that the chief religious festivals take place. With decreasing frequency and increasing regularity of occurrence comes at the same time an increase in elaborateness of form. Where in a hunting group the favor of the gods is sought by means of a feast differing little from the ordinary social gatherings of friends, in the agricultural community the same end must be sought through a comparatively elaborate religious festival, marked by a considerable amount of form and ritual.

In connection with the religious observances of the typical communal clan, there arises a special class of persons charged with the management of the seasonal festivals. This body, in arranging the calendar of the year, grows comparatively learned in such simple scientific laws as are of importance to the agriculturist; thus there comes into existence a distinct priesthood, whose recognized function is to carry on the religious life of the community, and to direct to a certain extent the conduct of economic operations. As time goes on, these men are regarded not only as knowing, but also as controlling the workings of natural forces. In the hunting tribe, each medicine-man obtains a certain power over the clan, as a result of his supposed influence with some special divinity; but the priesthood in the agricultural society forms an organized body, arrogating to itself the power of controlling natural forces in general: as a consequence, the claim of the jugglers, though temporarily it may stand side by side with that of the priesthood, finally goes down before the latter, and the priestly body stands forth as an autocratic power in the community.

To recapitulate: the hunter's religion is a polytheism in which the chief gods are animal types and such natural forces as are most manifestly of influence upon animal and human life: in an agricultural society plant deities take the chief place, and at the same time there is a more developed worship of the productive powers of nature and of atmospheric phenomena: among hunters, religious ceremonies are frequent, but exceedingly simple; among agriculturists, they are less frequent, but more regular and formal: the republican clan carries on its own worship without the intervention of a third party, although it may look to the sorcerers for information in certain emergencies: the communal clan is characterized by the presence of a priesthood which takes upon itself the general direction of all religious and even of economic activities.

In each of the culture stages outlined above, the natural conservatism of religious feeling may cause the preservation of many deities and ceremonies whose genesis is to be traced to economic conditions long since past. A study of a people whose religion is characterized by such features gives much satisfactory evidence of the truth of the theory postulating the economic antecedents of religion. There is other proof, however, which is even more convincing. This proof is to be found in the analysis of the religion of a people whose economy is in a transitional state. In such a society, if the hypothesis is correct, religious thought will be found undergoing a transitional process corresponding to that taking place in the manner and methods of production; and hence features of religion characteristic of both the older and newer economy, will sometimes stand forth with almost equal prominence. That the Iroquois economy was in such a transitional state is a fact too familiar to need repetition. The real question is whether their economic development was reflected in the growth of their religious conceptions.

Many of the more modern writers ascribe to the Iroquois a comparatively well-developed monotheistic conception of God.[1] On the other hand, the Jesuit missionaries, who knew them best, and the more careful investigations of the present day, unite in contradicting any such assertion. Le Jeune, for instance, says of the Hurons: "They have neither sought nor recognized him (God) except on the surface of created things, in which they have hoped for happiness, or dreaded some misfortune."[2] What Le Jeune says of the Hurons seems to have been true also of the Five Nations. All these tribes had many divinities of divers sorts; each divinity owing its origin to some aspect of the economic relationship between man and his environment.

The tendency towards fetishism, so strong among domestic economists, was still to a certain degree apparent in the Iroquois religion. The Iroquois were likely to regard all things animate

[1] Schoolcraft, "Hist. Ind. Tribes," I, 31, 32, 35; Morgan, "League," 149 sq.; Chadwick, "People of the Longhouse," pp. 134 sq.

[2] Jes. Rel., X, 159. Cf. Lloyd, notes to Morgan's "League" (ed. 1901), II, 333–335. Compare with this the statement of the Sack chief (Jes. Rel., LVII, 283): "We care very little whether it be the devil or God who gives us food. We dream sometimes of one thing, sometimes of another; and whatever may appear to us in our sleep, we believe that it is the manitou in whose honor the feast must be given, for he gives us food; he makes us successful in fishing, hunting, and all our undertakings."

Cf. Also the Jesuits' assertion in regard to the Missisakiks (Jes. Rel., LV, 221): "Their training and the necessity of seeking their livelihood have reduced them to such a condition that all their reasoning does not go beyond what relates to the health of their bodies, and the success of their hunting and fishing, and good fortune in trade and in war. And all these things are, as it were, so many axioms from which they draw all their conclusions—not only as regards their residence, occupations, and manner of acting, but even as regards their superstitions and divinities."

Of the Illinois, a tribe whose civilization was very like that of the Iroquois, the Jesuit Relation says (Jes. Rel., LXVI, 233): "As all their knowledge is limited to the knowledge of animals and of the needs of life, so it is to these things that all their worship is limited."

and inanimate as possessing an intelligence similar to their own; to anything, therefore, which for the moment seemed capable of helping or hindering them, they were ready to give presents and address conciliatory and friendly speeches. Of the Hurons, one of the Jesuits says: "They address themselves to the Earth, to Rivers, to Lakes, to dangerous Rocks, . . . and believe that all these things are animate."[1] On the way to Quebec particular rocks were often invoked by the Hurons.[2] Among the Five Nations the same custom prevailed in regard to the rocks along certain routes.[3] In general, however, individuals of any particular class of objects were not regarded as supernatural beings, but rather as reasonable persons, to be treated like ordinary men. As an example of this, there may be cited an occurrence among the Pottawatamies on Green Bay. A young man of this tribe was killed by a bear. Thereupon, his friends and relatives made war on the bears, killing five hundred, "as satisfaction for the death of that young man who had been so cruelly treated by one of their nation."[4]

Notwithstanding this tendency towards fetishism, the Iroquois inclined more and more to the worship of types or abstractions of classes of objects or beings, than to the adoration of individual specimens. Their life as hunters had changed their religion from a mere fetishism to a fairly well developed polytheism. Their hunting life, in the first place, had led to the apotheosis of various animal species. Every species of animal was supposed to have a great progenitor or "elder brother, who is, as it were, the source and origin of all individuals, and this elder brother is wonderfully great and powerful."[5] To see one of these in a dream meant luck in hunting. Besides cherishing a general respect for all animal species, each Iroquois gens,[6] furthermore, chose a particular one as

[1] Jes. Rel., X, 159. Cf. Jes. Rel., X, 167; VIII, 121; LXVIII, 47.

[2] Jes. Rel., X, 165.

[3] Jes. Rel., XLIV, 25-27. Cf. V, 285; XIII, 270-271; XXXIII, 225.

[4] Jes. Rel., LX, 153.

[5] Powell, "Wyandot Gov't," Eth. Rep., 1879-1880, p. 65; Chadwick, "People of the Longhouse," pp. 83-84.

[6] The Ball gens is an apparent exception. But this group was probably a subdivision of the "Small Turtle." See Chadwick, "People of the Longhouse," p. 84.

its special symbol and tutelary god. These divinities represented classes of animals of use in satisfying vital wants, or else having some less direct influence, beneficial or otherwise, upon economic welfare. The Iroquois legend of the origin of gentile totems probably tells the exact truth in the matter. Mrs. Smith, in her paper on "Myths of the Iroquois," relates as follows: "Later, as the numerous families became scattered over the state, some lived in localities where the bear was the principal game, and were called from that circumstance the clan of the Bear. Others lived where the beavers were trapped, and they were called the Beaver clan. For similar reasons, the Snipe, Deer, Wolf, Tortoise, and Eel clans received their appelations."[1] Not only each gens, but also each village possessed its special symbol and tutelary divinity, quite unconnected with the gentile totems.[2] Every individual, likewise, had his tutelary demon, to which none was more devoted than the hunter, who, having made his selection, after retirement into the forest, rigorous fasting, and observance of dreams,[3] thenceforth during his life offered to this special divinity prayers and sacrifices through means of various symbols which he considered appropriate.[4]

Just as hunting life had caused the apotheosis of certain animal species, so the growing importance of agriculture among the Iroquois led gradually to the deification of those plants upon which the people depended for vegetable food. The most prominent of these divinities were the spirits of maize, of beans, and of pumpkins. These were called "The Three Sisters," and were the objects of special reverence. Other spirits, even to that of the strawberry, were also worshipped, and thanked for their services.[5]

The adoration of plant life was common to all the Iroquois settlements. Plant deities differed from animal deities, however,

[1] Smith, "Myths of the Iroquois," Eth. Rep., 1880–1881, p. 76. *Ibid.*, p. 77.—Some gentes even went to the length of claiming these divinities as their own ancestors. Cf. Lloÿd, Morgan's "League," II, 218. (Ed. 1901.)

[2] Chadwick, "People of the Longhouse," p. 85.

[3] Lafitau, I, Jes. Rel., XIII, 270; LVII, 277.

[4] Cf. Jes. Rel., LVII, 277.

[5] Payne, "History of America," I, 464, note 1.

in this: individuals, gentes, and villages,—all chose certain animals as objects of their special worship; whereas plants were worshipped by all alike. This will appear strange when it is remembered that the Iroquois were at the time of the Discovery, even more dependent on agriculture than on hunting for a livelihood. The reason for the predominance of animal deities may probably be found in the undeniable conservatism of religion. Agriculture, as the newer manner of production, had as yet failed to dislodge the older divinities of the hunting life from their topmost place in the scale of importance. Eventually, if Iroquois civilization had been allowed to grow on undisturbed, we might have found new settlements taking maize or the bean or the pumpkin, instead of the bear or the wolf or the deer, as their tutelary divinity.

The Iroquois worshipped not only the spirits of plants and animals representing the direct sources of their supply, but also the more conspicuous natural phenomena influencing their welfare. The sky, the sun, the rejuvenating power of nature, rain, and warm winds were adored as blessing-bringing deities; frost, hail, and cold winds were propitiated as harbingers of evil.

The sky and the sun would naturally be regarded as divine powers by the most primitive people. Without air and light and warmth, it was perfectly obvious that both they and all animals and plants would perish: hence they came vaguely to regard sky and sun as creating and ruling over all living things. Le Clerq says that the Gaspesiens, a wild forest hunting and fishing tribe near the mouth of the St. Lawrence, worshipped the sun as the author of all things. At dawn and at dusk they came out of their cabins, turned their faces toward the sun, and saluting with voice and gesture, made a prayer for prosperity in war and in hunting and fishing, for health for themselves and their families, etc.[1] The Souriquois, a Nova Scotian tribe, also believed in a god whom they called by the same name as the sun and whom they invoked in times of great need, saying, 'Our Sun, or our God, give us something to eat."[2] These nomad hunters,

[1] Le Clercq, 165 sq.

[2] Jes. Rel., III, 133. Cf. Accounts of Quebec Indians: Jes. Rel., IV, 203; V, 35; 153, note 41. Also Jes. Rel., VI, 161, 163, 173; XXXIX, 15;

however, had but very indistinct ideas of the divinities they invoked. Had the Iroquois remained merely hunters and warriors, their notions might have been no less faint and obscure. But to them as semi-agriculturists, the vital importance of sunlight, air and moisture was ever increasingly apparent. Whether a summer was warm or cool, cloudy or clear, whether frosts came early or late, was of immensely greater importance to them as agriculturists than as hunters. Hence the Iroquois had formed some fairly clear conceptions of the different supernatural beings in whom they saw personified the several phenomena so influential in their economic life, and around these deities they had assembled a well developed series of legends and beliefs.

The foremost of the Iroquois divinities was the Sky, personified as Taronhiawagon, the Holder of the Heavens and the Master of Life, declaring his will in dreams.[1] To the Hurons, the Sky was "a power which rules the seasons of the years, which holds in check the winds and waves of the sea, which can render favorable the course of their voyages and assist them in every time of need."[2] If a man was drowned, if an unseasonable frost injured the maize crop, the Hurons believed that it was all due to the anger of the Sky. To both Hurons and Iroquois proper, the Sky tended to take the place corresponding to that of Jove in Greek mythology.

Agreskoui, the other great divinity of the Iroquois proper, seems to have been a personification of the Sun, as distinct from the Sky. Agreskoui was also regarded as a god whose influence was to be felt on every side. He, too, like Taronhiawagon was called "Master of Life," and continually invoked "in the forests and during the chase, on the waters and when in danger of shipwreck." To him the first fruits of every enterprise were always

L, 285; Perrot, Ch. 5, notes, p. 276; Schoolcraft, "Hist. Ind. Tribes," V, 64; La Potherie, I, 121.

[1] Jes. Rel., X, 323; LIV, 65; LV, 61; VIII, note 36. Hale, "Iroquois Book of Rites," in Brinton's "Library of Aboriginal American Literature," No. 2, p. 74. Parkman, "Jesuits in North America," Vol. I, Introd., p. lxxvii.

[2] Jes. Rel., 161 sq.

offered.[1] Warriors, too, regarded the sun as their special god, and occasionally offered him the flesh of captives.[2]

Taronhiawagon and Agreskoui, however much the conception of them may have been clarified by the agricultural experience of the Iroquois, were evidently personifications of the sky and the sun, which took their rise primarily in the mind of the hunter and warrior. The forces of nature manifesting themselves especially in regeneration, growth, and prosperity in both animal and vegetable life, seem to have been personified in Jouskeha, a god of Huron origin, but venerated by all the Iroquois. Most investigators regard the adoration of Jouskeha as simply another aspect of sun-worship. Mr. Hewitt, on the other hand, insists that Jouskeha represented not the sun in particular, but the reproductive and rejuvenating powers of nature.[3] The Iroquois legends themselves are somewhat obscure on this point. The version cited by Mr. Hewitt makes Jouskeha the grandson of Eyatahentsic, the wife of Taronhiawagon. According to this account, Jouskeha is the grandson of the Sky and of the Earth, and has nothing in particular to do with the Sun. But whether Jouskeha is regarded as simply another personification of the powers centered in the Sun, or whether it is believed that he represented to the Iroquois something quite distinct from the

[1] Jes. Rel., V, 286; XXXIII, 225; XXXIX, 207; LIII, 225; LVII, 97. Parkman, "Jesuits in North America," Vol. I, Introd., p. lxxvii.

[2] Subordinate to the sun in this capacity were two other war gods. Among the Iroquois the subordinate deity was Echo. This God, according to Mrs. Smith, "only exercised his power during their wars with other tribes, in which by repeating among the hills their cries of Go-weh, he insured their almost certain victory. He was even honored with special Thanksgiving. ("Mythology of Iroquois," Eth. Rep., 1880–1881, p. 52.)

The Hurons recognized another god of war. This deity, Le Jeune says: ". . . they imagine as a little dwarf . . . he appears to many when they are on the point of going to war. He caresses some—a sign—that they will return victorious; others he strikes upon the forehead, and these can truly say that they will not go to war without losing their lives. (Jes. Rel., X, 183.)

[3] Hewitt, "Cosmogonic Gods of the Iroquois," American Assoc. Adv. Sci. Proc., 1895, pp. 241–250.

Sun, is really not a matter of great moment. The essential point is that in Jouskeha the Iroquois evidently embodied those mysterious forces of reproduction and growth, whose importance, though perceptible to him as a hunter, became increasingly obvious as he came to depend more and more upon agriculture as the source of his food supply. Jouskeha was *par excellence* the beloved and beneficent deity of the Hurons and Iroquois.[1] He created the earth and everything in it. To his activity were due the lakes and streams with their fish, the woods with their game, and the fields with their crops of maize and pumpkins. He sent the refreshing showers and the warmth necessary for the growth of plants. To him, also, mankind owed the knowledge of fire. Like a man he grew old, but in a moment he could rejuvenate himself, and become a young man of twenty or thirty years; thus, though to some extent subject to the weaknesses of humanity, Jouskeha never died. To him no prayers or sacrifices were made, since his benevolent nature demanded no propitiation.[2]

[1] Jes. Rel., V, 285, 286; VIII, 117, 303; X, 129, 133, 135 sq., 323; XLII, 149; Perrot, "Mémoires," n. 161 (Tailhan). Parkman, "Jesuits in North America," Vol. I, Introd., pp. lxxv–lxxvii.

[2] "Moreover, they esteem themselves greatly obliged to this personage; for, in the first place, according to the opinion of some—without him we would not have so many fine rivers, and so many beautiful lakes. In the beginning of the world, they say, the earth was dry and arid; all the waters were collected under the armpit of a large frog, so that Jouskeha could not have a drop except through its agency. One day, he resolved to deliver himself and all his posterity from this servitude; and in order to obtain this, he made an incision under the armpit, whence the waters came forth in such abundance that they spread throughout the whole earth, and hence the origin of rivers, lakes, and seas. . . . They hold also that without Jouskeha their kettles would not boil, as he learned from the Turtle the process of making fire. Were it not for him, they would not have such good hunting and would not have so much ease in capturing animals in the chase, as they now have. For they believe that animals were not at liberty from the beginning of the world, but that they were shut up in a great cavern, where Jouskeha guarded them. . . . However, one day he determined to give them liberty in order that they might multiply and fill the forests,—in such a way, nevertheless, that he might easily dispose of them when it should seem good to him. This is

In Nature, it is obvious even to the savage eye that a constant struggle goes on between positive and negative forces. Hence as in Jouskeha the Iroquois reverenced the productive and rejuvenating power in Nature; so in Ataentsic, his mother—or according to some legends, his grandmother—and in Tawiscara, his twin brother, they embodied their fear of the destructive elements which so often spoiled their hunting and ruined their crops. According to Mr. Hewitt's version of the tale, Ataentsic, the wife of Taronhiwagon, fell from the sky upon the back of a turtle. where she gave birth to a daughter, who in turn gave birth to twin sons, Jouskeha and Tawiscara. Ataentsic, Mr. Hewitt thinks, is a personification of the night and the earth, while her daughter is to be identified with the moon. Other legends, however, contain no mention of Ataentsic's daughter, but make Ataentsic herself the mother of Jouskeha and Tawiscara, and the personification of the moon. In any case, Ataentsic is generally regarded as the goddess of disease and death: Tawiscara, with whom Jouskeha carried on a mortal struggle, represents all that is destructive in frost, hail, ice, etc. In all that the latter did, he was aided by Ataentsic. The idea of the powers of disease, death, and night combining with the powers of cold and dampness to work destruction to life on the earth would arise naturally in the savage mind. As Mr. Hewitt says, "the effects of frost and cold are best seen in the morning, when the god of ice and

what he did to accomplish his end. In the order in which they came from the cave, he wounded them all in the foot with an arrow. However, the Wolf escaped the shot; hence, they say, they have great difficulty in catching him in the chase.

They pass yet beyond this, and regard him as profane Antiquity once did Ceres. According to their story, it is Jouskeha who gives them the wheat they eat; it is he who makes it grow and brings it to maturity. If they see their fields verdant in the Spring, if they reap good and abundant harvests, and if their Cabins are crammed with ears of corn, they owe it to Jouskeha. I do not know what God has in store for us this year; but to judge from the reports going round, we are threatened in earnest with a great scarcity. Jouskeha, it is reported, has been seen quite dejected, and thin as a skeleton, with a poor ear of corn in his hand."—Jes. Rel., X, pp. 135 sq.

cold has accomplished his nefarious work under cover of darkness."

Though the conception of the creative and destructive forces in nature as supernatural beings, was evidently clarified and extended by agricultural life, it seems to have proceeded originally from hunting experience. On the other hand, certain specific phenomena seem to have been deified by the Iroquois purely as a consequence of their increasing attention to agriculture. The chief of these were rain, and the west and north winds. Summer showers so necessary for a successful harvest, and often coming in the shape of thunder storms, were worshipped in the person of He-no, the Thunderer. This god the Iroquois always called "grandfather." They invoked him at seed time and rendered him public thanksgiving at the Harvest celebration. The west wind was revered as the brother of He-no, since the two together brought rain. The north wind, on the other hand, which often brought frost to kill the unripe corn, was feared and propitiated as an evil deity.[1] The earth, though perhaps in the purely hunting stage identified to some extent with Ataentsic, the evil deity, gradually, as the Iroquois depended more and more upon the food produced by their fields, came to be reverenced as their mother and bountiful benefactor. "We return thanks," ran the Seneca prayer, "to our mother, the earth, which sustains us."[2]

It seems clear, then, that the religion of the Iroquois was not monotheistic in character. Neither was it marked by a well developed polytheistic hierarchy, such as is characteristic of a nation in which the religion of one group has been superimposed upon that of another, a conquered people. In fact, the Iroquois creed acknowledged but a simple polytheism, in which many divinities stand side by side, each claiming a certain amount of veneration from the savage worshipper. In their nature and attributes, these deities reflect the transitional state of the Iroquois economy. It must be remembered that a part of the Iroquois population still consisted of hunters and warriors;

[1] Morgan, "League," pp. 149 sq.; Smith, "Myths of the Iroquois," Eth. Rep., 1880–'81, p. 154.

[2] Morgan, "League," pp. 219–221.

this fact, taken together with that of the conservatism of religious tradition, accounts for the prominence of deities whose origin must be traced to the wants and satisfactions of the hunting life: yet, undoubtedly, many of these conceptions had been changed and extended as a result of the growing importance of cultivated plants in the estimation of the Iroquois. Furthermore, certain deities, the worship of which goes back to an exclusively agricultural origin, had been added to the already existing group, as the result of years of maize culture on the part of a portion of the population. In the case of the Iroquois, therefore, it seems justifiable to assert that the nature of the deities they worshipped was the logical outcome of the manner in which they carried on production.

The ceremonies by which the Iroquois deities were worshipped are to be classified under as many headings as the deities themselves; that is to say, there is one form of worship which was universally accorded to the hunting divinities; another sort which belonged primarily to those connected with agriculture.

The religious rites observed by the Iroquois, as hunters, were frequent and simple. Hunters and warriors pursue their calling practically all the year round, and so feel more or less constantly their dependence upon the powers governing their economic welfare. As the conception of the importance of these deities was extended under the influence of agricultural life, the frequency of these ceremonies increased, until almost every activity of individuals or villages was accompanied by some act of worship. Among the Hurons, writes a Jesuit father, ". . . their remedies for diseases; their greatest amusements when in good health; their fishing, their hunting, and their trading; the success of their crops, of their wars, and of their council;—almost all abound in diabolical ceremonies."[1] Hardly any feast was held at which some tobacco or fat was not thrown into the fire as a mark of respect to some deity or deities.[2] Most of these offerings were to the Sky and Sun. Among the Hurons a sacrifice of tobacco was made to the Sky for a successful maize crop, and to the

[1] Jes. Rel., XXVIII, 53.

[2] Jes. Rel., X, 159, 324; XXXIX, 13; LI, 183.

Sun and Moon for success in war and hunting[1] The Iroquois proper were in the habit[2] of taking the leg of a deer or bear or some other wild beast, rubbing it with fat, and throwing it on the fire; at the same time praying the sun to accept their offering, to light their paths, to lead them and give them victory over their enemies, to make their corn grow, and to give them a successful hunting or fishing season. To Agreskoui, some of the flesh of the first deer killed on the hunt, or of the first fish caught by the fishing expedition was dedicated by the Iroquois.[3] Tobacco and game, however, were not the only offerings made to the Sky and Sun. According to Lafitau,[4] "Our Iroquois sometimes place in the open air, on top of their cabins, branches and collars of percelaine, clusters of their Indian corn, and even animals that they consecrate to the Sun." The Jesuit Relations testify, further, to the fact of occasional human sacrifices to Agreskoui in his capacity of War God. On one occasion, a female captive was killed, while "an old man cried in a loud voice, 'Aireskoi, we sacrifice to thee this victim that thou mayest satisfy thyself with her flesh, and give us victory over our enemies.'"[5] As a general rule, however, human sacrifices did not occur in Iroquois worship. Offerings for the most part consisted of meat, maize, tobacco and wampum, and were made at pleasure by any who so desired. Besides sacrifices, the Iroquois used dances and feasts as a means of propitiating supernatural powers. Among the Hurons, especially, nearly all formal dances were essentially religious rites, abounding in ceremonies.[6] Feasts for religious purposes were constantly being given,—for instance, to restore virtue to a charm supposed to bring good luck in hunting, or to effect the cure of the sick.[7] Fasting, as well as feasting, played no small part in the life of

[1] Jes. Rel., XXIII, 55; LVIII, 181.

[2] Carr, "Mounds," Sm. Inst. Rep., 1891, p. 551. Cf. Jes. Rel., X, 159; XXXIX, 13.

[3] Jes. Rel., XXXIX, 209.

[4] Lafitau, I, 179. Cf. Jes. Rel., XLII, 197.

[5] Jes. Rel., XXXIX, 219; cf. Jes. Rel., XIX, 71.

[6] Jes. Rel., XVII, 129, 163, 155-157.

[7] Jes. Rel., X, 209; XX, 51; XVII, 209; XIV, 61 sq.; LVII, 123; LX, 187.

the Iroquois hunter and warrior. The practice of fasting was based partly on the idea of propitiating the gods by such a sacrifice of personal comfort in their honor: but the main cause of its continuance was probably the dreams and visions which naturally resulted from excitement and weakness induced by starvation. The object was to bring favorable dreams, and give the power of seeing and understanding things above the ordinary comprehension. Long fasts were thus often undertaken to insure luck in games, in hunting, and in war.[1] All these sacrifices, feasts, dances and fasts, it must be remembered, took place at any time that it pleased an individual or a group, or seemed to be advisable for the welfare of the community. This sort of worship, characteristic of the religion of a hunting people, was quite impromptu, and was constantly going on.

Maize culture, and the rise of religious conceptions based on agricultural experiences, led to the institution among the Iroquois of a new and additional series of religious observances. Certain great festivals were now held in honor of the plant deities and the forces influencing plant life. Owing to the very nature of the agricultural life, with its fixed seasons devoted to sowing, cultivation and harvest, the festivals celebrating these important events took on a fixed and regular character and were conducted according to a comparatively formal ritual. Of the six or eight great annual religious festivals of this nature, the most important were the Planting, the Green-corn and the Harvest celebrations. The celebration held in spring at the corn-planting season lasted for seven days, each day occupied with a regular program of feasts, dances, and ceremonies of various sorts. Their object was in the main to invoke the gods for the success of the crop.[2] The Green-corn festival followed next in order of importance. This, too, lasted several days, and was marked by a regular succession of prayers, dances and feasts. It was a time of thanksgiving " to our mother, the earth, which sustains us, to the corn and to her sisters, the beans and the squashes, which give us

[1] Jes. Rel., X, 189, 199, 203–205, 207; XII, 69; XXIII, 155; LVII, 273.

[2] Morgan, "League," pp. 193, 196; Smith, "Myths of the Iroquois," Eth. Rep., 1880–'81, p. 115.

life, . . . to the sun . . . that he looked upon the earth with a beneficent eye. . . ." This was the gala season of the Indian year.[1] Another festival took place at the time of the final harvest, when the ripe corn was gathered in. The Indian name of this feast signified "thanksgiving to our supporters" [the corn, the bean and the squash].[2] The celebration lasted four days, and was a time of general rejoicing. Similar festivals, though of less duration, celebrated the coming of the maple sugar and strawberry seasons.[3]

It is clear that the existence of two sets of deities, the one hunting, the other agricultural, led to the rise of two varieties of religious observances. The one, characteristic of the hunting life, was marked by few ceremonies, and was almost constantly in evidence; the other was the outgrowth of agricultural conditions. Worship, in the latter case, was carried on by means of festivals occurring at fixed and relatively far distant intervals, and characterized by a considerable amount of formality.

For purposes of worship, the organization of the Iroquois was still largely that characteristic of the republican clan. All worship except that of the tutelary divinity of each person was carried on, not by the individual, but by the economic organization to which he belonged. In religion, as in production, the individual Iroquois enjoyed no great importance. Feasts, dances, and rites of any great significance, were carried on by the gens, the village, or the whole tribe, according as the object to be accomplished was more or less local;[4] in an act, therefore, of propitiation or thanksgiving in which the whole village was interested, the affair became one of general participation. In such events all the gentes were likely to take part, the members of each wear-

[1] Carr, "Mounds," Sm. Inst. Rep., 1891, p. 551; Morgan, "League," pp. 198 sq.; Smith, "Myths of the Iroquois," Eth. Rep., 1880–1881, p. 115. The Green-corn festival of the Iroquois was the less developed form of the Great Feast of the Busk observed by the Gulf State Indians.

[2] Morgan, "League," pp. 206–207; Smith, "Myths of the Iroquois," Eth. Rep., 1880–1881, p. 115.

[3] Morgan, "League," pp. 187, 197.

[4] Morgan, "Anc. Soc.," p. 82; Powell, "Wyandot Gov't," Eth. Rep., 1879–1880, pp. 64, 65; Jes. Rel., XLII, 197.

ing the peculiar adornments of the gens, such as tatooed designs, chaplets, and ornaments of various sorts; the ceremonies being arranged and directed by the chiefs, who found such duties not the least onerous of those connected with their office;[1] and thus the clans and villages under the direction of their chiefs carried on the religious as well as the productive activities of the community.

Yet, there were, at the same time, indications of the development of a priestly order such as is usual in the typical communal clan. Mr. Morgan says that for the management of the great agricultural festivals there was associated with the chiefs a body of people called "Keepers of the Faith."[2] These were equal in number with the chiefs, and were elected by each gens, just as were the chiefs. After their election, they were installed with suitable ceremonies by the tribal council, and given new names significant of their office. Men and women were chosen in about equal numbers, the females being charged with the duty of preparing the food consumed at the festivals. It was not possible to refuse the office, but after a reasonable period of service, the incumbent might resign, dropping his official name and resuming the one he originally bore. Consequently, though the ceremonies attendant upon hunting life demanded the creation of no special officials, the greater regularity of agricultural life resulted in the rise of a set body of a quasi-priestly character. These Keepers of the Faith, however, were as yet merely elected representatives of the clan; and hence one is justified in concluding that among the Iroquois, the organization of worshippers was identical with that already in existence for purposes of production.

The secret societies of the Iroquois were perhaps merely an extra manifestation of the spirit of clan and tribal worship. Their relation to the latter organizations, however, is not entirely clear. Perhaps it may be concluded with Mr. Morgan, that there was one such society in each phratry.[3] Apparently, how-

[1] Jes. Rel., X, 231; XVII, 201; XXIII, 109, 185, 243; XXVI, 265; XXVIII, 87.

[2] Morgan, "Anc. Soc.," p. 82, note 2.

[3] Morgan, "Anc. Soc.," p. 97. The phratry, a subdivision of the Iroquois population becoming prominent only in religious and social life.

ever, not everybody in the phratry belonged to the society. In these associations men and women seem to have been on an equal footing, all being under oath to keep secret the mysteries of the organization. Each society had its own dances and ceremonies which it performed upon request for the cure of the sick and for other like purposes.[1] Anyone who had been the object of one of these rites thenceforward belonged to the fraternity by which it had been performed. Le Jeune tells of a Huron who upon the manifestation of certain symptoms was "declared to belong entirely to the Brotherhood of Lunatics . . .; the remedy which is used in this disease . . . is the dance they call Otakrendorae; the brethren they call Atirenda."[2]

Of all the organizations hitherto spoken of not one professed to exist for any other purpose than that of worship. Propitiation and praise were their functions, and they did not profess to have any special means of knowing the will of the gods. This latter power, on the contrary, was supposed to belong to individuals, especially to those gifted ones known as sorcerers, jugglers, or medicine men.

Every adult Iroquois regarded his or her dreams as special messages sent by Taronhiawagon and the multitude of dream spirits subordinate to him.[3] If a hunter dreamed that a feast was necessary in order to insure a good hunting season, he would inform the chiefs and instantly the whole machinery of the community would be set in motion and a great feast given. Any one who refused to carry out a dream, even though it concerned only the welfare of the individual dreamer, "draws upon himself the hatred of all the dreamer's relatives, and exposes himself to feel the effects of their anger."[4] The Hurons were even more super-

Each tribe had two phratries, made up of several gentes, probably all subdivisions of an original gens.

Cf. Powell, "Wyandot Gov't," Eth. Rep., 1879–1880, pp. 60 sq.; Morgan, "Anc. Soc.," pp. 90–101.

[1] Jes. Rel., XXX, 23; LXIII, 306; XVII, 197.

[2] Jes. Rel., X, 207.

[3] Jes. Rel., LIV, 65, 97, 99.

[4] Jes. Rel., LII, 125. Cf. Jes. Rel., LV, 61. At midwinter an annual festival was held in honor of dreams. This was a time of license and

stitious in regard to their dreams than were the Iroquois proper. Of them La Jeune says: "The dream is the oracle that all these poor people consult and listen to, the Prophet which predicts to them future events, the Cassandra which warns them of misfortunes that threaten them, the usual Physician in their sicknesses, the Esculapius and Galen of the whole country,— the most absolute master they have. If a captain speaks one way and a dream another, the captain might shout his head off in vain,—the dream is first obeyed."[1] Sorcerers, among both Iroquois and Hurons, were individuals gifted with especial powers of dreaming and of otherwise finding out the desires of the gods and of influencing their actions.[2] These sorcerers were probably men and women constitutionally fitted to endure long fasts and vigils, and who consequently had vivid dreams; at the same time, they were undoubtedly persons of superior intellect who had gained much empirical knowledge through observation of what went on around them. The result was that they gained great power over their less intelligent or less well-informed fellow clans-people. Some of them even went so far as to claim that they themselves were divinities.[3] Whether they aspired to be considered divine, or merely friends of the gods, they undoubtedly held a superior place in the community. A class standing between the clans and the sources of the surplus, on account of their supposed influence with the supernatural powers controlling that surplus, they must be treated as an organization outside of the clan, both from the economic and from the religious point of view.

Sorcerers usually claimed preeminence as belonging to one of three classes; they might be prophets or seers; they might be masters of the elements; or they might be healers of diseases.[4]

confusion, when everyone tried to guess everyone else's dreams and soul desires. A general interchange of property often resulted.

Cf. Smith, "Myths of the Iroquois," Eth. Rep., 1880–1881, pp. 112–118; Morgan, "League," p. 207.

[1] Jes. Rel., X, 169, sq. Cf. XV, 177; XXXIII, 189 sq.

[2] Jes. Rel., X, 197; XVII, 195; XIX, 171; XXXIX, 21; XXXIII, 193; VIII, 125, 261.

[3] Jes. Rel., X, 205.

[4] Jes. Rel., X, 193–195.—"There are among these people men who presume to command the rain and winds; others to predict future events;

The predictors of future events, especially those who were skillful in foretelling the results of war and in discovering the size and position of hostile bands, had considerable influence in time of war.[3] In seasons of drought, especially in the sandy Huron country, where rain for the corn-fields was needed every other day, those sorcerers who professed to be masters of the elements and to be able to bring rain were the most powerful persons in the community. There was no limit to the servile obedience that a well-known rain-maker could exact from the whole country-side in return for his services at such times.[2] But according to Le Jeune and to most other witnesses, the busiest and most powerful among the sorcerers were those who pretended to be able to cure the sick by means of their magic arts.[1] In the clan economy, where everyone takes part in production, no misfortune is more frequent or more dreaded than illness and helplessness. Any ailment not obviously due to some natural cause was supposed to find its origin in some unsatisfied desire of the patient's soul, or in some evil spell or charm. Now the sorcerer was the only physician who could find out the nature of either of these causes of disease, and cure the patient;[4] hence this class of magicians was a large and influential one. In a previous chapter, the place these doctors occupied in the distributive system of the Iroquois, and the amount of tribute that they exacted from the common clans-people in return for their services has been spoken of. All the above mentioned sorcerers were regarded as public benefactors, and were highly honored and respected. Of the opposite class of magicians—the malignant witches and wizards—

others to find things that are lost; and lastly, others to restore health to the sick."

[1] Jes. Rel., XIX, 83; XXVI, 175.

[2] Jes. Rel., X, 35 sq. Cf. XXIII, 55.

[3] Jes. Rel., XIII, 203; XXXIX, 17, 21; XL, 239. Cf. Ch. V, General Culture.

[4] These doctors were divided into two classes: (*a*) Those who diagnosed the case, discovering the cause of the illness by means of pyromanchy, feasts, dances, etc., and (*b*) those who endeavored to cure the disease by incantations, potions, blowing, etc. Cf. Jes. Rel., VIII, 123; XIII, 33; XVII, 213; XV, 179; XXX, 199 sq.

mention has been made in a previous chapter.[1] They were believed to practice their arts in secret and always with malevolent intentions. They were accused of having power to cause death and disease, to blast the crops, to bring bad weather, etc. Mary Jemison says that great numbers of persons of both sexes were put to death upon this charge.[2]

To be brief, the religion of the Iroquois was that of a tribe of hunters upon which was being gradually super-imposed the beliefs and ceremonies characteristic of an agricultural community. They feared or revered the objects of utility or disutility to them in their hunting life, the different animal species, and also the natural phenomena—the sky, the sun and moon, the waters and winds—which seemed to influence their existence. In all this, they did not differ essentially from their nomadic hunting neighbors to the north of them. But agriculture had brought with it an increased reverence for the sky and the sun, the wind and rain, shown in the greater clearness and definiteness of their mythology as compared with that of the northern forest tribes. It had also added to the occasional and irregular ceremonies characteristic of the purely hunting tribe, certain set and regular observances celebrating the important dates of the agricultural year. As yet there was not much development of a priesthood beyond that characteristic of the hunting stage; but the growth of the agricultural clan and the settlement of the people in permanent villages caused worship to be more regularly carried on by the clans, as such, with more formality, and with the aid of a certain number of specially delegated officials. Over these worshipping communities the sorcerer, as revealer of the divine will, gained more power than he could have had over the small and changing groups of the hunting tribe. The Iroquois and the Hurons, therefore, furnish a striking example of the religious life of the hunting tribe in process of transformation into that characteristic of a typical agricultural community.

[1] See Chapter II, State and Government.

[2] "Life of Mary Jemison," pp. 182–183. Cf. Jes. Rel., XXXIII, 217 sq.

CHAPTER IV.

MORALS.

The Religious beliefs of the Iroquois had little or no bearing upon their moral code. To quote from Mr. Lloyd: "The beautiful and elevating conception of the Great Spirit watching over his red children from the heavens, and pleased with their good deeds, their prayers and their sacrifices, has been known to the Indians only since the Gospel of Christ was preached to them. . . . In the early days the various divinities were simply powers to be propitiated, but of influence on conduct and morals, there was not much more in the Indian belief and observances than in a gambler's charms for luck."[1] The Indians' code of morality was, in fact, the direct outcome of their life as hunters and warriors and primitive agriculturists. In their estimation, manly virtue meant any qualities that tended to make good hunters and warriors; virtue in women was synonymous with skill in agriculture and housekeeping; and virtue in general meant the possession of qualities likely to fit an individual of either sex for usefulness as a clan member. It came about, therefore, that the ideal man of the Iroquois was, above all things, brave and daring; at the same time, also, he possessed fortitude, patience and self-control. On the other hand, industry, economy, patience, and prolificness were the chief virtues of the ideal woman.

The clan system of organization necessitated the presence of certain qualities in all the members of the community. The fact that every individual member of a clan was dependent for his own well being upon the prosperity of the organization caused the idealization of the virtues of hospitality, truthfulness, honesty, and chastity in the ordinary life of all persons within the village. Hospitality was taken for granted, since in reality all property within the clan was common, and only possessed by individuals

[1] Morgan's "League" (ed. 1901), Appendix, II, pp. 333–335.

for convenience's sake. Theft was unnecessary and ridiculous, since any one could have what he wanted, if he would take the trouble to ask for it. Lying, between brothers and allies, could not be tolerated, since the whole efficacy of the clan organization depended upon the existence of a perfect understanding among its members. Thus all these virtues, so strong among the Iroquois, were either natural consequents of clan life, or necessitated in order to keep up a strong organization.

Another virtue of the Iroquois—respect for old age—seems to have been the result of the double clan life. In the purely nomadic existence of the Algonquin forest hunter, where only the able-bodied and young could endure the long journeys, and where food was often scarce, it was considered at times a filial duty to put to death the old and helpless.[1] Among the Iroquois, on the contrary, agricultural pursuits and a settled life in permanent villages gave assurance of peace and plenty; the experienced advice of the aged, furthermore, was valuable to both warriors and agriculturists: hence old age was revered and cherished.

The same ethical code which demanded truthfulness, hospitality and generosity to some of their fellows, countenanced and even exacted in the conduct of the Iroquois toward others any amount of cruelty, deception, and treachery. The clan system of organization, in fact, gave rise to a two sided morality. Within the clan and village all was kindness and brotherly love; without its limits, every man's hand was against every man. The Jesuit accounts of the treatment of condemned captives in the Iroquois villages are simply blood-curdling in their horrible details. The very man who would cheerfully give his last morsel of food to a starving fellow clansman would take the greatest pleasure in tormenting by the hour some helpless stranger, or assassinating him from ambush. Nevertheless, it was this very pitilessness which strengthened the clan in the eyes of its neighbors, and permitted its success in the hard struggle for existence.

Briefly, then, among the Iroquois, a good hunter and warrior, hospitable, truthful, and honest in his relations with his fellows, was considered a man of ideal character. Similarly a woman

[1] Lafitau, I, 490.

who was a good farmer, housekeeper and mother, fulfilled her whole duty in life. Outside their own society none of these virtues was required. Treachery, murder, and theft in dealing with tribes not in alliance with their own, the Iroquois considered perfectly legitimate. This whole moral code is, as has been pointed out, directly traceable to the economic conditions under which the Iroquois carried on their struggle for existence.[1]

[1] Jes. Rel., VIII, 127; X, 175; XXXVIII, 267; LXIII, 201. Lafitau, I, 583. Schoolcraft, "Hist. Ind. Tribes," III, 190, 191. Chadwick, "People of the Longhouse," pp. 122, 123 sq. La Hontan, "Voyages," II, 110.

CHAPTER V.

THE GENERAL CULTURE OF THE IROQUOIS.

Economic conditions, it has been demonstrated, explain the peculiarities of the family, the state and government, and the religion of the Iroquois. Finally, it is evident that to their life as hunters, or as agriculturists, or as both, may be traced the most striking features of their general culture.

Active life in the open air, the severe military training, and the temperance and self-control necessary in the life of the good hunter and warrior,—all contributed to make the Iroquois, physically, fine specimens of humanity. The men were tall, often six feet in height, well proportioned, with regular features and comparatively light complexions.[1] The Hurons, too, were "all well made men of splendid figures, tall, powerful, good-natured, and ablebodied."[2] "Their senses," the Jesuit says, "are most perfect, . . . they have exceedingly acute vision, excellent hearing, an ear for music, and a rare sense of smell. With this sense they frequently discover fire long before seeing it."[3] Lafitau adds his testimony to that of the author just quoted. Their sense of orientation, he says, was remarkably strong. It was aided by observation of the trees, whose tops in that region generally lean toward the south, and whose bark is thicker on the north side than on the south.

The observation of the heavenly bodies for purposes of orientation on the hunt or on the war path had led to a certain amount of astronomical knowledge.[5] The Iroquois distinguished between different constellations, and recognized that the stars had a fixed

[1] Jes. Rel., LVIII, 263.
[2] Jes. Rel., VI, 25.
[3] Jes. Rel., XXXVIII, 259.
[4] Lafitau, II, 240.
[5] Morgan, "League," pp. 441–442; Lafitau, II, 235 sq.

relation to each other as far as position was concerned. Runners of the Confederacy in autumn and winter directed their course by observation of the Pleiades. They called the group "Te Iiennonniakoua"; *i. e.* The Dancers. In spring and summer, they took as their guide another group—four stars at the angles of a rhombus, which they called the Loon. The Polar Star was, however, their main guide on their journeys. "They call the Polar Star 'Iateonattenties' (the star which never moves). . . . It is this polar star which directs them in their journeys," says Lafitau. Venus, or the Morning Star, they knew and called "Te Ouentenhaouitlia" (She brings the day). The Milky Way they called "The Road of Souls." The Great Bear was also recognized by the Iroquois, and called, curiously enough, the Bear—(Okonari). In short, the Iroquois may be said to have known just as much siderial astronomy as was useful to them as hunters and warriors: further knowledge they neither needed nor possessed.

The needs of their life as hunters and warriors, determined also the limits of the Iroquois medical learning. Since feeble members of the population were not likely to survive the period of infancy, and since there was but little opportunity to nurse and care for any one seriously ill; the Iroquois confined their attention to those suffering from simple and temporary maladies, or from injuries whose cause and cure were not difficult to ascertain. Hence a knowledge of the efficacy of certain roots and herbs in curing wounds and simple diseases was all that they possessed of the science of medicine.[1] In the preparation and use of these simple natural remedies certain persons were more skilled than others, but as yet no special class of physicians had been formed. The Iroquois apothecary was, in fact, a hunter and warrior, or an agriculturist like any other clan member.

Some slight knowledge of certain great natural laws had been gained by the Iroquois as a result of agricultural experience.

[1] Complicated diseases were handed over to the sorcerer to be cured by magic arts. Jes. Rel., XIII, 27, note 3; XVII, 211 sq.; XXXIII, 203. The principle of the Turkish bath; *i. e.* the sweat-lodge, was the remedy most frequently used for simple ailments. Lafitau, II, 371–372, 374.

Although not yet an exclusively maize-growing people, they nevertheless were dependent enough upon their crops not only to feel the effect of the law of diminishing returns of land, but also to make intelligent efforts to hinder its working. There is considerable evidence that they understood and put into practice the principle of the rotation of crops,—sowing beans, for instance, in a field where corn had been grown the previous year.[1] Probably, like the New England Indians, they also recognized the necessity of letting worn out fields lie fallow for a year or two before re-sowing.[2] To what extent the Iroquois understood the value of fertilizers does not seem clear. Most writers say nothing about the matter; which silence, together with the fact that the village had to move to new lands every dozen or so years, leads to the conclusion that very little was done in this direction. The practice of burning over the fields every autumn, preparatory to sowing in the spring,[3] undoubtedly enriched the ground; but the farmers themselves probably thought of it chiefly as an easy way of clearing the ground of stubble, weeds, and brush, rather than as a means of fertilizing the soil. Lescarbot, however, in speaking generally of the Indians of the Atlantic Coast, says that they fertilize their fields with shells;[4] and Hennepin says explicitly[5] that the Iroquois were no exception to the rule. "The Iroquois," he says, "manure a great deal of ground for sowing their Indian corn." It seems likely that the Iroquois had some idea of intensive methods of agriculture, though this was not yet sufficiently developed to allow them permanently to use the same fields. Such extended knowledge was, in fact, not yet necessary. The Iroquois had plenty of room in which to move about; they used

[1] La Potherie, III, 18–19.

[2] Champlain, p. 84—"Il y avait aussi plusieurs champs qui n'étaient point cultivés, d'autant qu'ils laissent reposer les terres; et quand il y veuleut semer, ils mettent le feu dans les herbes, et puis labourent avec leurs bêches de bois."

[3] Beauchamp, N. Y. St. Mus. Bul., No. 16, p. 54.

[4] Lescarbot, II, 834.—"Tous ces peuples engraissent leurs champs de coquillages de poissons."

[5] Hennepin, "A New Discovery of a Vast Country in America," I, 18 (London, 1698).

a great deal of wood for fuel, and so found it convenient to go from place to place in order always to be near an abundant supply; and lastly, their hunting and fishing habits made them not averse to changing their location as game grew scarce near the old site.

The fact that they were partly a hunting and partly an agricultural people accounts for the double basis upon which the Iroquois formed their calendar. Much of the activity of the hunter and warrior is carried on at night, when the stars are the travellers' sign posts;[1] furthermore, the hunting season is a comparatively elastic period, not compressed absolutely into a few months, but extended more or less throughout a large part of the year: therefore hunters adopt the simple and obvious method of computing time by nights rather than by days, and by lunar months rather than by the movement of the earth around the sun. Agriculturists, however, carry on their labors only by day, and during a fixed period of the year; to them the solstices and the succession of the seasons in which field operations go on or are intermitted, are facts of primary importance: hence, while the hunter divides the year into lunar months, the agriculturist divides it into seasons, reckoned according to a solar calendar. The Iroquois, as might be expected, used both the sun and the moon calendar. In ordinary affairs of hunting, fishing, and war, they computed time by nights and lunar months, twelve "moons" making up their year: but for purposes of agriculture, they also reckoned by seasons, marking their recurrence by great festivals. According to Lafitau,[2] they sometimes reckoned by solar months, for which

[1] Schoolcraft, "Hist. Ind. Tribes," V, 171.

[2] Lafitau, II, 225 sq. "Ils comptent ordinairement par les nuits. . . . Plûtôt que par les jours; par les mois lunaires plûtôt que par ceux du soleil. . . . Cependant cette manière de compter est subordonnée au cours du soleil, qui sert a regler leurs années, les quelles sont partagées en quatre saisons comme les notres, et sont divisées en douze mois. La manière de compter par les lunes, n'est pas même si universelle, qu'ils ne comptent aussi par les années solaires. Je crois avoir remarqué que l'une et l'autre manière de compter est affectée à certaines choses, et qu'en d'autres occasions elles s'employent indifférement. . . . Les années solaires sont destinées à marquer l'âge des hommes. . . . Ils comptent de la même façon pour toutes les choses éloignées, qui renferment une période de temps assez longue. . . . Ils comptent au contraire par les Lunes et par les nuits,

they had a special word, quite distinct from the word used to designate a lunar month. Moreover, the names of their months from spring to fall were based upon the operations involved in sowing, growth, and harvest. Thus, in their method of computing the passage of time, as in many other respects, the Iroquois "halted" between two opinions, the one characteristic of the hunter, the other of the agriculturist.

In short, the Iroquois manner of production; *i. e.* forest hunting and fishing, together with maize-culture, though it had developed physically and mentally a fine type of humanity, had neither necessitated nor encouraged any great progress in scientific learning. A little astronomy—enough to guide them in their journeys, and to make up their yearly calendar, a slight knowledge of the healing art, a certain degree of intelligence in regard to the laws governing plant life, was all that they needed to aid them in the process of utilization, as they carried it on.

Although the hunting and fishing life of the Iroquois and their primitive form of agriculture had brought about among them only a slight development of scientific knowledge, yet their method of production; *i. e.* the clan organization, had encouraged a decided growth in literary culture, and in social customs and observances.

The well organized political and military system of the Iroquois demanded some means of conveying information otherwise than orally, and also of preserving a record of transactions and events otherwise than by mere tradition. These objects were accomplished by pictography and by the use of strings of wampum. Neither invention was peculiar to the Iroquois, any more than to

quand il s'agit d'un terme assez court, de prendre leurs mesures pour leurs voyages de guerre, de chasse, ou de pêche, pour leurs rendez-vous, et pour le temps de leur retour, etc. Dans ces occasions là même ils disent fort bien, "Skarakouat," qui signifie un mois héliaque, comme s'Ouennitat qui signifie un mois lunaire, mais le premier est moins ordinaire que le second."

Of La Hontan's account of the intercalation of an extra month every thirty years—"la Lune perdue,"—Lafitau says, "Tout ce la me paraît être la pure invention de cet auteur. . . . Ce qu'il y a de certain, c'est qu'ils n'ont point une exactitude mathématique pour les intercalations, et pour accorder les années héliaques avec les années lunaires."

any other tribe in North America. But the more complex and closely organized the group, the more necessary becomes some method of intercommunication and of record-keeping. Hence the clan, tribal, and confederate form of the Iroquois state, demanded and brought about a greater development along these lines than was necessary among domestic economists.

Pictography, the more primitive of the two methods, was used mainly by the older and more primitive of the clan organizations, namely, that of the warriors. By this means they conveyed information and kept memoranda of their different expeditions. A party of warriors in the course of a journey were accustomed here and there to remove some of the bark from a tree, and draw on the exposed surface certain significant designs. To the initiated passer-by those rough pictures revealed, for instance, the number of days the party had been travelling, the route taken, and the number of prisoners.[1] A permanent history of warlike events was kept in a similar manner. Mary Jemison says: "In order to commemorate great events and preserve the chronology of them, the war chief in each tribe (gens) keeps a war post. This post is a peeled stick of timber ten or twelve feet high that is erected in the town. For a campaign, they make, or rather the chief makes, a perpendicular red mark about three inches long, and half an inch wide; on the opposite side from this, for a scalp, they make a red cross, thus ‡; on another side, for a prisoner taken alive, they make a red cross, in this manner X, with a head or dot; and by placing such significant hieroglyphics in so conspicuous a situation, they are enabled to ascertain with greater certainty the time and circumstance of past events."[2] This method of recording, however, seems to have been confined purely to military affairs. For civil matters, a more developed system was in vogue, namely, that based upon the use of wampum or little sticks of wood.

The date of the introduction of shell wampum records among the Iroquois has been a matter of some dispute. Mr. Morgan regards it as a prehistoric occurrence. He says, "the original wampum of the Iroquois, in which the laws of the league were

[1] Jes. Rel., XII, 215; Doc. Hist. N. Y., I, 7 sq.

[2] "Life of Mary Jemison," p. 71.

recorded, was made of spiral fresh-water shells . . . which were strung on deer-skin strings, or sinew, and the strands braided into belts, or simply united into strings."[1] Mr. Hale and Mr. Beauchamp, however, are of the opinion that it was not until the coming of the whites and their tools that wampum was used by the Iroquois for the purpose of keeping records. Previous to that time most of their shell wampum had been used as ornaments, while collections of little sticks served as memoranda of events. Mr. Hale's and Mr. Beauchamp's opinion in the matter is supported by the testimony of Loskiel,[2] who says: "Before the Europeans came to North America, the Indians used to make their strings of wampum chiefly of small pieces of wood of equal size, stained with black or white. Few were made of mussels, which were esteemed very valuable and difficult to make; for not having proper tools, they spent much time in finishing them, and yet their work had a clumsy appearance. But the Europeans soon continued to make strings of wampum, both neat and elegant, in abundance. These they bartered with the Indians for other goods. . . . The Indians immediately gave up the use of the old wooden substitute for wampum, and procured those made of mussels, which though fallen in price, were always considered valuable."

Even after the coming of the whites, sticks continued to be used to some extent, at any rate among the Hurons. Le Jeune speaks of the chiefs' "packages of council sticks, which are all the books and papers of the country:"[3] and in another place we are told that "The captains use little sticks instead of books, which they sometimes mark with certain signs, sometimes not. By the aid of these they can repeat the names of a hundred or more presents, the decisions adopted in the councils, and a thousand other particulars which we could not remember without writing."[4]

[1] Morgan, "League," p. 120, note.

[2] Hale, "Indian Wampum Records," in Pop. Sci. Mo., L, 481–483; Beauchamp, "Iroquois Trail," p. 63. Cf. Beauchamp, N. Y. St. Mus. Bul., No. 41—"Wampum and Shell Articles." Holmes, Eth. Rep., 1880–1881, pp. 240 sq.

[3] Jes. Rel., X, 293.

[4] Jes. Rel., XXXVIII, 261.

As a general thing, however, after the coming of the Europeans, shell wampum was employed by the Iroquois for mnemonic purposes. Lafitau says that the little cylindrical tubes were used in two forms,—as "branches" and as "collars." The former were made of cylinders of white wampum, strung together. They were used in unimportant affairs. The so-called "collars" were large belts made of strings of white and of purple wampum, the different strands being fastened together by leather bands. The length and width of the belts and the kind of wampum used were determined by the importance of the affair in hand. Ordinary belts were of eleven strands, each of one hundred and forty pieces of wampum. In general, the colors used, the arrangement and relative position of the strands,—all denoted some special event or transaction, and its important details.[1]

No written contract could have been more binding, nor sworn oath more solemn, than the strings of wampum given to each other by parties concerned in a transaction, as a witness and record of what had passed between them.[2] The law held equally good in intercourse between different clans or gentes, villages, and tribes. "For all these peoples," the Jesuit Relations say, "have no voice except it be accompanied by presents; these serve as contracts, and as public proofs which are handed down to posterity and attest what has been done in any matter."[3] These records, so unintelligible to white men, were absolutely clear and unmistakable to those among the Iroquois whose task it was to read them. La Hontan says, "The savages have the best memories in the world. They remember so far back that when our governors . . . propose to them things contrary to what has been proposed to them thirty or forty years ago, they answer that the Frenchmen are contradicting themselves, . . . and in order to confirm their response more strongly, they have the porcelain collars brought out that were given them at that time. For these are a sort of contracts . . . without which it is impossible to settle any affair of importance with the savages."[4]

[1] Lafitau, I, 503–508.
[2] Jes. Rel., XXII, 311; XXV, 53; XXXI, 87; LIII, 187.
[3] Jes. Rel., XXII, 291; XXXIII, 133; XL, 165.
[4] La Hontan, "Voyages," II, 109.

Altogether, although they had no alphabet, nor any kind of written language, the Iroquois had a pretty complete system of signs—pictorial and otherwise—by the aid of which they conveyed information and recorded events. Their method was not original with them, but was used to a greater or less degree by most of the other tribes of North America. As the Iroquois had developed it, however, the system exactly met the needs of their simple life, and satisfied them as well as more elaborate methods satisfy people at a more complex stage of culture.

To the clan organization of the Iroquois may also be attributed the great amount of social intercourse, the dances, feasts, and games, which resulted in the development among them of a remarkable degree of tact, ease of manner, and conversational ability. The perpetual council meetings also worked toward this end. Aside from the councils, however, dances, feasts, and games, either religious or purely social in their object, were constantly occurring among the Iroquois. There were many different dances; some of them performed by small and select bands, some exclusively for women, others for warriors, and many of them open to all.[1] Dialogues were a regular part of some dances, and formed a fine training in the art of repartee and impromptu speaking. Often a dancer picked out a certain individual among the spectators, and ridiculed him amid the laughter and applause of all. Sometimes young men ranged themselves in two opposite lines, and each one made fun of his vis-a-vis until one or the other gave up the contest.[2] Similarly, feasts and games cultivated the social abilities of the Iroquois clansfolk.

The possession of a comparatively large agricultural surplus, their general prosperity and consequent leisure time, gave the Iroquois an opportunity to cultivate a certain degree of esthetic taste. Undoubtedly, from the standpoint of modern civilization, it was a comparatively slight development. In regard to the sense of smell, for instance, they had not gone beyond the stage reached by the most primitive utilitarian. According to the statement of one of the Jesuits: "They are indifferent to the

[1] Morgan, "League," pp. 261, 268 sq., 279, 283 sq.; Lafitau, I, 521 sq.; Jes. Rel., VIII, 29; XVI, 65; XL, 209; LXI, 111, 119.

[2] Lafitau, I, 525, 526.

odors of things which are not eatable."[1] Nevertheless, along artistic lines, the Iroquois had made considerable advance, especially in regard to the decoration of clothing and utensils. Loskiel says that in matters of dress the Iroquois set the fashion for the neighboring tribes, having means and leisure for this, as well as high rank.[2] The festal costumes of the Iroquois were elaborately decorated with embroidery and dyes of various colors. In decorating skins, they took great pains, first cutting in the desired outlines, then coloring with paints made from certain red earth found on the shores of lakes and rivers, and also with juices and ashes of plants.[3] Leggings were often embroidered with elk hair dyed red or yellow and trimmed with a fringe of porcupine quills, stained scarlet.[4] Other garments also were often beautified in this way. Their tools and utensils were also often elaborately decorated; for instance, on the handles of wooden ladles were sometimes carved human figures, animals, etc. In general, the Iroquois displayed much taste and ingenuity in this sort of ornamentation.[5]

In conclusion, one is justified in ascribing to economic conditions among the Iroquois the origin of the chief features of their general culture and intelligence. Their manner of production, on the one hand, accounts for the extent of their knowledge of certain sciences and natural laws, and also for their method of computing time: on the other hand, their methods of production explain the development of their system of communication and record-keeping, and of their social life and its consequent characteristics: finally, their general economic prosperity accounts for their preëminence along artistic lines. In short, the general culture of the Iroquois was neither greater nor less in extent than might have been deduced from a knowledge of their economic situation.

[1] Cf. ante, p. 263, note 2.

[2] Beauchamp, "Iroquois Trail," p. 118. Cf. Lafitau, II, 54 sq., 58; Jes. Rel., LXII, 179; XXXVIII, 249.

[3] Lafitau, II, 33, 35.

[4] Jes. Rel., LXVIII, 265; LXIV, 293.

[5] Morgan, "League," p. 383; Holmes, Eth. Rep., 1880–1881, p. 230.

BIBLIOGRAPHY.

I. Early French Missionaries and Explorers.

The Jesuit Relations and Allied Documents.

Travels and Explorations of the Jesuit Missionaries in New France, 1610–1791. (73 vols.) Edited by Reuben Gold Thwaites. Cleveland, The Burrows Brothers Co. MDCCCXCVI.

"Lettres édifiantes et curieuses écrites des Missions étrangères par quelques Missionaries de la Compagnie de Jesus." Paris, 1712–1736. 23 vols.

Boucher. "Histoire véritable et naturelle des Moeurs et Productions du Pays de la Nouvelle France, vulgairement dite le Canada." Paris, 1664.

Champlain. "Voyages de la Nouvelle France." Paris, 1632.

Charlevoix. "Histoire et Description Générale de la Nouvelle France." Paris, 1774.

De Laët. "Novus Orbus, seu descriptionis Indiae Occidentalis libri, XVIII." French trans. Elzevir, 1640.

Citry de la Guette. "Histoire de la Conquête de la Floride." Paris, 1665.

Hennepin. "Description de la Louisiane." Paris, 1683.

"A New Discovery of a Vast Country in America." London, 1698.

Lafitau. "Moeurs des Sauvages Amériquains." Paris, 1724.

La Hontan. Tome Premier; "Nouveaux Voyages de . . . dans l'Amérique Septentrionale."

Tome Second; "Mémoires de l'Amérique Septentrionale; ou, La Suite des Voyages de M. le Baron de La Hontan." La Haye, MDCCIII.

La Potherie. "Histoire de l'Amérique Septentrionale." Paris, 1722.

Le Clercq. "Nouvelle Relation de la Gaspesie, qui contient les Moeurs et la Religion des Sauvages Gaspesiens." Paris, 1691.

Lescarbot. "Histoire de la Nouvelle France." Paris, 1609.

Margry. "Mémoires et Documents." Paris, 1679.

Perrot. "Mémoire sur les Moeurs des Sauvages de l'Amérique Septentrionale." Ed. by Tailhan. Paris et Leipzig, 1864.

Sagard. "Histoire du Canada." Paris, 1686.

Thévenot. "Recueil des Voyages." Paris, 1687.

II. English and Other Sources.

Bancroft, Hubert Howe. "Native Races of the Pacific States." San Francisco, 1886. 5 vols.

Barton, George A. "A Sketch of Semitic Origins." New York, London, 1902.

Bartram, John. "Observations on the Inhabitants, Climate, Soil, Rivers, Productions, and other Matters worthy of Notice, made by Mr. John Bartram in his travels from Pennsylvania to Onondaga, etc." London, 1751. (Reprint, Rochester, 1895.)

Beauchamp, W. M. "The Origin of the Iroquois." Amer. Antiq., Vol. XVI, p. 61.

"The Iroquois Trail, or Footprints of the Six Nations in Customs, Traditions and History." Fayetteville, N. Y., 1892.

"Wampum Belts of the Six Nations." Amer. Antiq., II, 228.

N. Y. State Museum Bulletins; 1897–1903.

No. 16. "Aboriginal Chipped Stone Implements of New York."

No. 18. "Polished Stone Articles used by the New York Aborigines before and during European Occupation."

No. 22. "Earthenware of the New York Aborigines."

No. 32. "Aboriginal Occupation of New York."

No. 41. "Wampum and Shell Articles used by the New York Indians."

No. 50. "Horn and Shoe Implements of the New York Indians."

No. 55. "Metallic Implements of the New York Indians."

Bücher, Dr. Karl. "Die Entstehung der Volkswirtschaft." Tübingen, 1901.

Carr, L. "Mounds of the Mississippi Valley." Report of the Smithsonian Institute, 1891, p. 507.

Colden. "History of the Five Nations." London, 1747.

Documentary History of New York. Albany, 1849, 1850.

Vol. I, p. 11. "Observations of Wentworth Greenhalgh."

Vol. III, p. 3. "Champlain's Expeditions."

Hale, H. "Indian Wampum Records." Popular Science Monthly, 1897, Vol. L, p. 481.

"The Iroquois Book of Rites." In Brinton's Library of Aboriginal American Literature, No. II, 1883.

Harvey, H. "History of the Shawnee Indians." Cincinnati, 1855.

Heckewelder, John. "Manners and Customs of the Indian Nations." Amer. Phil. Soc. Trans., Vol. 1, p. 1.

Hewitt, J. N. B. "The Cosmogonic Gods of the Iroquois." Proc. Amer. Association Adv. Sci., 1895, p. 241.

Holmes, W. H. Report of the Bureau of Ethnology.
1880–1881, p. 185. "Art in Shell of the Ancient Americans."
1891–1892, p. 3. "Prehistoric Textile Arts of Eastern U. S."

Life of Mary Jemison. New York, 1856.

Jenks, A. E. "Faith as a Factor in the Economic Life of the Amerind." Amer. Anthrop., 1900, Vol. II, No. 4, p. 676.

Keasbey, L. M. "The Institution of Society." Internat. Monthly, 1900, I, 355.
"Prestige Value." Q. J. Econ., 1903, Vol. XVII, p. 456.
"A Classification of Economies." Proc. Amer. Philosophical Society, 1902, Vol. XLI, No. 169.

Loskiel. "Mission of the United Brethren among the Indians of North America." London, 1794.

Mason, Otis. "Origins of Inventions." New York, 1895.

Marshall, O. H. "The First Visit of De la Salle to the Senecas, made in 1669." Buffalo, 1874.

Morgan, L. H. "League of the Ho-de-no-san-nee, or Iroquois." Rochester, 1851. New York, 1901. Edited by H. M. Lloyd. 2 vols.
"Houses and Houselife of the American Aborigines." U. S. Geog. and Geol. Surveys Contrib. to American Ethnology, IV. Washington, 1881.
"Ancient Society." New York, 1877.

Parkman. "The Jesuits in North America." Boston, 1890.

Payne, E. J. "History of America." Oxford, 1899. 2 vols.

Powell, J. W. Report of the Bureau of Ethnology.
1881–1882, p. xxxviii. "Kinship and the Tribe; Kinship and the Clan."
1879–1880, p. 57. "Wyandot Government."

Ruttenber, E. M. "History of the Indian Tribes of Hudson's River." Albany, 1872.

Schoolcraft. "Notes on the Iroquois." New York, 1846.
"History of the Indian Tribes." Philadelphia, 1851–1857. 6 vols.

Shea, J. G. "Historical Sketch of the Tionontates, or Dinondadies, now called Wyandots." Historical Magazine, 1861, V. 262.

Smith (Erminie). "Myths of the Iroquois." Report of the Bureau of Ethnology, 1880–1881, p. 51.

Woodward. "Wampum; a paper presented to the Numismatic and Antiquarian Society of Philadelphia." Albany, 1878.

Maps, Ethnolog. Report, 1885–1886. N. Y. State Museum Bulletins, No. 31; No. 32. 1900.
Jesuit Relations, Vol. 1.
Morgan. "League of the Iroquois." New Edition, 1901.

CPSIA information can be obtained
at www.ICGtesting.com
Printed in the USA
LVHW041735210623
750386LV00002B/320